A COMPACT TEXTBOOK OF WESTERN POL. THOUGHT

notionpress.com

A COMPACT TEXTBOOK OF WESTERN POL. THOUGHT

Dr. Th. Siamkhum

notionpress.com

Notion Press

5 Muthu Kalathy Street, Triplicane,

Chennai - 600 005

First Published by Notion Press 2013

ISBN: 978-93-83416-23-3

FOREWORD/ ACKNOWLEDGEMENT

'A compact Text Book of Western Political Thought' authored by Dr. Th. Siamkhum, Associate Professor of Political Science, Churachandpur College is, exclusively meant for BA 2ND Semester Students of Political Science under Manipur University. It is strictly a syllabus based text book on Western Political Thought for the Affiliated Colleges of Manipur University.

It is my sincere belief that the book, the first of its kind, would best serve the interest of those students for whom it is written and published.

I wish the book a grand success.

Dated: Churachandpur

The 16th August, 2013

Sd/-

S.R. Gangte,

Head of Deptt. of Pol. Sc

Churachandpur College

CONTENTS

1

PLATO

A. Theory of Justice

Platonic theory of justice is an important contributory factor to the formation of the Ideal State of Plato 'The Republic' in which he discussed his theory of justice which is also sub-titled as 'Concerning Justice' is all about his theory of justice Plato, after discussing the then prevailing concept of justice in Greek, starts giving his own theory of justice. He rejected all the other contemporary concepts of justice in Greek.

After rejecting and discarding the then prevailing notions of justice, Plato gives his own concept of justice. According to his theory, justice resides both in individual and in the society. But, since Justice in the society or state exists in a more visible form, he tries to explain it with the help of state. According to him, like human mind state has three ingredients; reason, spirit and appetite which are represented by the rulers, soldiers and farmers respectively. All these three classes of people make valuable contributions for the creation of state; and justice could be realized only when all these three classes of people perform each of their function without interfering in the affair of others. Therefore, according to him, justice implies a sort of specialization of function, division of labour and a principle of non-interference and harmony.

Justice, he said, is a bond which holds a society together, a union of individuals, each of who has found his life work in accordance with his natural capacity and his training.

Platonic concept of justice is explained by Baker in the following words; "Social Justice may be defined as the principle of a society, consisting of different types of men who have combined under the impulse of their needs for another and by their combination in one society, and their concentration on their separate functions, have made a whole which is perfect because it is the product and the image of the whole of human mind. As the principle of such a society, it consists in the full discharge of each one of these types of the specific function for which, by its capacities, and by the place they have been given in society, it is naturally meant. Justice of state is the citizen's sense of duty of his station, issuing before the world in public action".

Plato's concept of justice has the following implications. In the first place, it implies functional specialization based on individual's capacity. In the second place, it implies non-interference in the sphere of other and concentration of one in one's station of life. The work of the ruler is to rule effectively and efficiently. He should not try to become a soldier or to become a farmer. In the same way, soldier or farmer should never try to become the ruler. The idea is, therefore, non-inference in the affairs of others. In the third place, it implies harmonous co-existence between the three classes of people. Finally, Plato's theory of Justice implies division of labour in a water-tight compartment. This is how he looks at justice in the context of state. Plato hold the view that when all of these classes of people in the society perform each of their duty efficiently and effectively, without interfering in the sphere of other, then only an ideal state would be created.

Plato also elaborates his concept of justice in relation to individuals. Justice with regard to individual, he said, implies a harmonious operation of each part of individual viz. reason, spirit and appetite. This makes the individual virtuous and social. He hold the view that if everyone devoted to the maximum to his duty, then ideal society will be established in which everyone will concentrate on his own sphere of duty and not meddle with the sphere of others. Plato claims that human behavior flow from three main sources: Desire (appetite), Emotion (Spirit) and Knowledge (intellect). These qualities are found in all human beings, but in different degrees. There are people, he said, who are embodiment of desires and who are naturally more interested in material prosperity than the other. These people are more efficient to take up trade and industry as their life profession. There are other groups of people who are full of emotion, courage, physical strength etc. They have enormous spirit and are naturally fit to be soldiers whose main duty is to protect the state from external invasions or internal disturbances. Finally, there are also a few exceptional people who are interested in meditation and understanding. This people have the knowledge, they have undergone along course of educational training. They are called philosopher kings. This group of a few intellectuals are to be the ruler of the state.

The central idea of Plato's theory of justice is that justice is for functional specialization for the harmonious development of state. Functional specialization could be achieved, he said, when each and every individual concentrate himself in his station of life. When an individual is put in a service where he is most suited for prolong period, he gains experience in due course, he becomes more efficient in his work. Therefore, he said, individuals must be mindful of his duty without interfering in the affairs of others who also have their own specialized professions. Justice, therefore, could be realized only when one concentrates in his work and not interfere in the affair of others. When there is justice in the society, then and there only an ideal state could be established where in each and every man could live a harmonous and happy life.

Criticism

Plato's concept of justice is not free from criticism. There are a number of critics right from his time till today. The followings are some of the major criticisms put forward by different writers.

In the first place, critics pointed out that Plato theory of justice is too much a moral principle which is in no way enforceable nor attainable. It is based on self-control for the interest of society. His concept of justice never perceives the possibility and the inevitability of clash of interest of individuals which is repugnant to the larger interest of society. Moreover, history testified that mere moral sanction has never been able to protect the social good.

In the second place, Plato's theory of justice emphasis on strict division of labour which is possible and viable only in Greek City state. In his contemporary Greek city state in which population was small, strict division of people into three professional classes might have been possible, but in present context, when population of even the smallest state is large and runs crores and millions, it is practically not possible to divide people into only three professional classes. Today, apart from the rulers, the soldiers and the farmers or traders, there are numerous groups of people engaged in numerous professions. Therefore, Plato's division of people into only three classes is no more relevant in our contemporary period.

In the third place, whilePlato accepted the endowment of men with three qualities viz. reason, spirit and appetite, he wants that individuals should devote himself to the development of only one faculty. He wants the rulers to develop their faculty of reason to the fullest possible extent while leaving the other two faculties – spirit and appetite undeveloped. This is certainly a lopsided development which is detrimental to harmonious growth of the state today. Therefore, his theory of justice based on lopsided development cannot be accepted as sound theory of justice.

In the fourth place, Plato wanted the philopher kings to be the rulers of the state by virtue of their knowledge and experience. But there is no absolute guarantee that the philosopher kings will always rule the state in the interest of the people as they too are just human beings having an inborn selfish interest, for man is naturally selfish. Moreover, Plato failed to realize that giving of absolute power to any person or group of persons, how morally and spiritually well trained they might be, is bound to lead to degeneration and corruption. Therefore, Plato's theory of justice which gives rulership entirely to philosopher kings cannot be regarded as a sound theory of justice.

In the fifth place, Plato's theory of justice gives rise to totalitarianism and ignores altogether humanitarian principles andequalities like equality, individualism and freedom. It is against the modern concept of democracy which guarantees equal rights and opportunities to every individual, irrespective of one's economic, social, educational and political position. Therefore, Plato's theory of justice which stratified people into three classes and which gives the right of rulership only to the philosopher king cannot be accepted as a sound theory of justice. It is, rather a theory of injustice rather than justice because it is doing much injustice to the soldiers and farming class who are deprived of their political right throughout their life.

In the sixth place, Plato subordinated individual to the state and reduced him to a mere means for the promotion of the interest of the state. He treats individuals only as an instrument for the promotion of the interest of the state. He bothers the least for the promotion of individual and his interest.

Finally, Plato's theory of justice is against the Marxian theory of classless society and most of the Marxists do not accept his division of people into different classes.

B.Plato's Scheme of Education

According to Plato, Education is an instrument for moral reform because education would reform and transform human soul. Education, according to him, inculcates sense of selfless service towards all and is, therefore, positive. Education helps one to perform his function efficiently and effectively and helps in the realization of social order. Barker said, "Education is an attempt to cure a mental malady by mental medicine" Plato believes that evils in the society could be eliminated through proper education, and therefore, considers it as a spiritual remedy.

Plato conceives that human soul was capable of living as long as it lives, and hence education is a life-long process. Knowledge was, therefore, to be acquired for the sake of perfection and excellence. To Plato, the mind was active, capable of becoming totally receptive to objects from the environment. Education, according to him reformed and established the right and congenial environment to ensure that the soul got attracted to things that were beautiful, and then moved towards beauty itself. Plato's theory of education, therefore, is primarily a reform of souls to perfection.

Scheme of Education

In the first place, Plato advocated for state control of education mainly because he wanted that all children must be given compulsory elementary education, which he believed, could be provided only by the state. His contention was that uneducated children were likely to be a liability for the state, and therefore, state should provide free and compulsory elementary education to all children, so that they may fully develop their mental faculties and becomes valuable assets for the state.

In the second place, Plato considered education as a positive means by which the ruler could mold the moral character of the people and promote spirit of unselfish devotion towards their duties. This is one of the reasons why he wanted state control of education

In the third place, Plato favors the inclusion of women in his scheme of education. He did not believe in the existence of distinction between men and women, and therefore, treated them equally. He even wanted that women should also hold public office if they were sufficiently educated.

In the fourth place, Plato was in favour of strict censorship of all literature to protect the youths from the influence of immoral character. He wanted that only the right and positive type of literature should reach the hands of the youths. The ruler who knows the best what is the wrong type, should check every piece of literature before it reaches the open market for sale.

In the fifth place, Plato's scheme of education aims at both moral and physical development. He holds the view that a healthy body produces a healthy soul. Therefore, to him education should develop both body and mind.

Finally, but most importantly Plato's scheme of education aims at production of philosopher kings who shall be the rulers of the state after a long and rigorous educational training.

CURRICULUM OF PLATO'S SCHEME OF EDUCATION

a) Elementary Education

Plato's elementary education could further be divided into three stages. The first stage, according to him, begins at the time a child was born and lasted up to the age of six years. During this period, both boys and girls should be given religious education. The second stage begins at the age of seven and ends at the age of 18. During this period student, both boys and girls are to be given training in music and gymnastic. Music was intended for the development of soul and gymnastic was intended for the development of body. The second stage would be entirely devoted for the harmonious development of body and soul. Gymnastic according to Plato, provides poise to feeling, and tempered spirits. It involved the training of the body for the sake of the mind. On the other hand, music was meant for softening of the spirit by developing the nascent power of reason. It includes the power of right opinion. The rhythm and diction of poetry, the sound of musical instrument, the shades, colours and shapes of art not only gave artistic sense, but also carried with it a moral principle of love for doing the right things. Music would uphold the social practice of each individual doing one work, without being a busy body. It was to instill a sense of simplicity, justice, conformity to a single principle and acceptance of a more cheerful life.

From the age of 18, there shall be two years compulsory military training. Two years compulsory military training will end at the age of 20. Those who could successfullycompleted two years of military training will become auxiliaries.

b) Higher Education

At the age of 20, a selection was made, and those who were selected would take up advance course in mathematics, which includes arithmetic, plane and solid geometry, astronomy and harmonics. According to Plato, arithmetic is necessary because it is pure intelligence for the attainment of truth, pure truth. To Plato, truth resides in thought. Apart from this, arithmetic also had a practical value like the use of number. Warriors and soldier need to learn the use of numbers for making proper and effective use of troops in wars. On the other hand geometry, according to Plato, helps in choice of positions and methods of tactics. Geometry also helps people to acquire the idea of good. Both astronomy and harmonics, serve the same purpose as arithmetic. The chief purpose of higher education, according to Plato, was to cultivate the spirit of free intellectual qualities.

Those who could not qualify this exclusive category of intellectuals would become soldiers who shall take the responsibility of defending the state from foreign aggression. They would be put in the second tier of ruling elite, next to philosopher king. The first stage in the scheme of higher education would last for 10 years from 20 to 30 years of age. At the age of 30 there would be another test and those who qualified in the test would study dialectic of metaphysics, logic and philosophy for the next 5 years (up to 35). They would study the idea of good and the first principle of being. They would receive some experience in the art of ruling. They would be put in the junior position in the military and political life of the state till the age of 35. Again, they would remain in this position for 15 years till the age of 50 years. At the age of the 50,Plato maintains that they would be fully equipped and spend their maximum time for contemplation and meditation. By this time because of their deep understanding of thing by virtue of their knowledge, they would be in a position to do only what is good for the community. Plato believes that only those who have the perfect knowledge should be entrusted to the rule of the state

To sum up Plato's scheme of education, we can say that the main aim of his scheme of education was perfection of human soul so that man is good. Right from the time when he was born, a child needs to be given education, first in religion. Religion, he believed is necessary to mold the moral character of a child. Then, he wanted all children, irrespective of their background, should be given compulsory elementary education up to the age of 18 years. He wanted that children, during this period be taught music and gymnastic; music for the development of young mind and gymnastic for the healthy growth of the body. He believes that the harmonious growth of soul and body is essential for the all-round development of a child.

The ultimate goal of Plato's theory of education, however, is to produce philosopher kings who have the outstanding knowledge in science, philosophy and dialectic. Philosopher kings of his scheme of education shall be the rulers of the state. According to him, philosopher kings are endowed with the highest kind of knowledge which enables them to know the full idea of good. Plato, therefore, believes that the philosopher kings, by virtue of their abundant knowledge would be capable of ruling for the good ofthe community as a whole.

Criticism

Plato's theory of education has been criticised by different writers at different times on the following grounds.

In the first place, critics pointed out that Plato's scheme of education was meant only for guardian class, and the bulk of citizens including artisans and peasants who constitute majority of the population were excluded. As a matter of fact, no system of education which excluded the larger section of the population could never be considered as a sound system of education.

In the second place, Plato's scheme of education was also criticized on the ground that it is too long a process. The rulers who have spent much a longer part of their life in their pursuit of education, become physically weak and would be incapable to rule effectively and efficiently. To become an effective ruler, one has to be physically fit as only knowledge without sufficient physical strength was unlikely to work.

In the third place, Plato's theory of education was also criticized on the ground that it overstressed the importance of theoretical perspective of education. A long 35 years theoretical training would hardly help one to deal with the reality of life. In order that education be effective, the scheme of education should include the practical aspect of education

In the fourth place, Plato's scheme of education advocated for state censorship of literature, which according to critics, would destroy the creative instinct of individuals, particularly the artists and poets.

In the fifth place, Plato's scheme of education is not logical. There is no continuity of his scheme of education. During the first stage he suggested the study of religious literature, during the second stage, he insisted the study of quite a different subjects – music and gymnastic which has nothing to do with religion. Then, during the third stage, he insisted on the study of science, arithmetics, geometry etc. which has nothing to do with music and gymnastic. It is, therefore, a disjointed education or fragmented education which would confuse the student at every stage.

In the sixth place, Plato scheme of education has been criticized for not making provision for education in the art of administration, which today constitutes one of the most important parts of education. The philosopher kings on whom the administration of the state is to be entrusted were not given any training in administrative education. It is highly doubtful that philosopher kings who are trained in music, gymnastic and dialectics would rule and administer the state effectively because the art of administration is not related to music, gymnastic or dialectics.

In the seventh place, Plato suggested for uniformity of curriculum for all people. There are different inborn talents and interests with every individual, and that to give the same kind of education, with the same kind of curriculum to these different individuals with diversified talents and interests, would not be the best kind of education. Children ought to be given training according to their talents and interest.

Plato's scheme of education, in spite of all these criticism, certainly was a big step toward educational improvement of Athen. He certainly deserves the credit for emphasizing that education must aim at both moral and physical development of individuals. He is the first philosopher who has given systematic scheme of education, and for that he deserves to be applauded by all those who love education.

c) Plato's Theory of Communism in Women

Plato's theory of communism was dominated by his conception of common ownership of wives and properties. It is also closely related to his theory of justice. In fact, communism was not unknown to Greeks. In Athen and Sparta, there existed some forms of communism like state control of private property. However, Plato was the first philosopher who developed the theory of communism of wives and of property based on political and psychological foundation. However, his theory of communism of wives and property was meant only for the guardian class and did not include other classes. The ultimate aim of Plato in developing his theory of communism of wives and property was that the guardian class which was entrusted to rule the state would be freed from problems related to family. His conception was that private property was the root cause of selfishness from which the ruler should be freed.

Plato, like Pythagoras, has the conception that men and women are equal in endowment and, therefore, should be treated equally. No distinction has to be made between them. Therefore, he suggested that once women completed higher education successfully, they could be included among the ruling elites and become legislators and rulers. In the Plato'sScheme of communism in women he suggested for reform in the conventional system of marriage and emancipation of women. For this, he suggested the abolition of the system of permanent marriage and establishment of private family. This, however, is meant only for women guardians.

According to Plato, conventional marriage inevitably subordinates women to men leading to subjugation and seclusion. Plato rejected the idea of marriage as a spiritual union of men and women based on love and mutual respect. He, however, agreed that marriage was necessary for reproduction and continuation of human race. Therefore, he suggested for temporary sexual union of men and women purely for the purpose of reproduction, that is, for bearing children for continuation of human generation.

Plato also suggested for strict regulation of sexual intercourse for reproduction. He was of the opinion that state should ensure the best and the fittest have the maximum sexual intercourse so as to produce the best human race. For this, he said, the Philosopher kings would decide on sexual union of men and women of guardian class.

To quote Plato "There would be as much union of the best sexes of both, and as few of the inferior as possible... no one, but the rulers know how this is being effected; otherwise our herd of Guardians may become rebellious. We must then institute certain festivals at which we shall bring together the bridges and the bridegrooms... The number of marriages we shall leave to the rulers'discretion ... I think they will have to invent some ingenious system of drawing lots, so that, at each pairing off, the inferior candidates may blame his luck rather than the rulers" (Plato page 1955:240)

According to Plato, the most ideal age for marriage was between 25 to 55 for men and 20 to 40 for women He was against equal relationship between mothers and sons and fathers and sons. The purpose of Plato's communism in women is not for encouraging sexual promiscuity, but rather for securing the best and most effective rulership. Regarding abortion, he said, it should be recommended for illegitimate mating and mating after the expiry of recommended age.

With regards to children born out of temporary marriage, he said, they should be left to the care of state preferably in state maintained nurseries. With the exception of philosopher ruler, no one would know the parentage of children. The idea was that if a parents did not know as to who was his child and a child would not know who were his parents, there could be equal love and affection to all children. Once both parents were freed from problems relating to family, they could devote all their times, energies and minds for common interest of the community.

Criticism

In the first place, Plato's theory of communism of women is criticized on the ground that he has gone too far on the organic conception of state. He treats state merely as an extension of family and makes no distinction between the two different institutions. In fact, state and family could not be treated as identical institutions in totality.

In the second place, sharing of common wives and common children is against morality and would lead to moral degeneration among the philosopher guardians which is against the healthy functioning of state administration.

In the third place, he said that children born out of common marriage would be taken care of by the state. But this proposition cannot be accepted for the healthy physical and moral growth of children. Children need fatherly love and care which they received in the family. But state may not be able to provide the same kind of love and affection which they could get from their parents in the family.

In the fourth place, it is totally unacceptable proposition that state should control mating of men and women. Plato, by proposing state control of mating reduces human beings to the status of animals.

In the fifth place, Plato treats the institution of marriage as a mechanical process. In fact, marriage is a social institution and its successful working depends largely on the proper understanding between husband and wife. It would be wrong and unfair to treat family only as a mating agency. Lastly, even if his theory of communism in women is found to be successful and workable, it is meant only for the guardian class which constitutes a small number of people and much a larger majority of people would be excluded in scheme.

However, in spite of all criticisms, Plato's theory of communism in women, could be considered as logical. He believes that an undivided loyalty to state could not be expected if guardians have family of their own. Guardian, if they have family would naturally give more loyalty to their families than the state which they ruled.

But it should be noted that his theory is highly unrealistic and devoid of hard realities of life.

d) Plato's conception of Communism in Property

Plato considered private property as the root cause all evils in the society. In order to root out evil in the society, he said, private property with its institution should be eliminated. He holds the opinion that possession of private property would give rise to selfishness and deviate the attention of philosopher kings from public service. He, therefore, suggested that the ruling philosopher kings should not possess private property, property which they could think theirs. To quote Plato, "To cure the greed of rulers there is no way short of denying them the right to call anything their own" He insists that the ruler should be confined in a common barracks, sharing common table and common meals. He thought that once philosopher kings have private properties or a property which he could call his, it would undermine the value of virtue which constitutes the most important possession of the ruling class. Once a person has property of his own, he would then be self-centred, greedy and selfish. Therefore, he said, no philosopher guardian should possess his personal property. However, it should be noted that his conception of communism of property is meant only for the philosopher kings, who according to him, are expected to thinks and concentrate only for the society and state which they ruled over. Therefore, philosopher kings should renounce property and family of their own.

Criticism

Plato's theory of communism in property has come under severe criticism on the following points.

Firstly, Plato's theory of communism is against the natural instinct of man. Possession of personal property is the natural will of man and to destroy the institution of private property is to destroy the natural instinct of man. Deprivation of individual property right is likely to do more harm than good for the development of society as a whole, because society is composition of individuals who have the natural desire to possess property which they can call, theirs. If individuals are deprived of property right as suggested by Plato, it will lead to lack of incentive to work hard which in turn will lead to lack of development for the society and state.

Secondly, Plato scheme of communism, both in women and property was meant only for the ruling elites and excluded workers, peasants and those who are engaged in other productive activities, who constitute majority of population. History is a witness that any scheme which excluded the majority of the population was bound to fail.

Thirdly, the abolition of property right to individuals is bound to adversely affect the spirit of charity and benevolence which are pre-requisite for the healthy growth of the society.

Fourthly, Plato's conception of communism in property is likely to result in the decrease of production. There will be less will to work hard, because even if individuals work they in and day out for maximization of production, there will be nothing which they could claim theirs. This is likely to adversely affect production processes leading to economics under-development.

Fifthly, Plato's theory of private property that is common ownership of property is against the accepted principle of liberty, equality and freedom and gives overcentralization of power and excessive state control of individual's life.

Finally, Plato's theory of communism was criticized by Aristotle and others for completely neglecting and marginalizing slaves, who constitute a signicant component of Greek population. Plato did not give any place for slaves who are, in fact, the backbone of Greek's economy.

e) Plato's Conception of the Rule of Philosopher Kings

Plato's conception of rule of philosopher king is based on his conception of human soul. Human soul, he said, is consisted of three elements – element of reason, element of spirit and element of appetite. According to him, out of these three elements; soul, element of reason is superior to the other two. Reason in man makes a man virtue, and the virtuous are those who have the knowledge and those who have the knowledge are considered wise and intelligent. Therefore, the ruler of the state must be those who are virtuous by virtue of their knowledge and wisdom. Plato said that the major cause of the prevailing turmoil in the state was that ignorant who were devoid of knowledge were ruling over the wise in the state. Plato opines that problems and turmoil's in the state could be solved only when the philosopher kings who received the perfect knowledge and wisdom after rigorous training were entrusted to rule the state... To quote him, "Until philosophers are kings or princes of this world have the spirit and power of philosophy, cities will never rest from their evils" His conception was that only competent and efficient people with sufficient knowledge and wisdom should have the right to govern.

There are some distinct features of Plato's conception of the rule of philosopher king which are discussed as follows:

The First distinct feature of Plato's conception of the rule of philosopher king was that it rejected democracy as the rule of ignorants which is most undesirable. On the other hand, he wanted the philosopher kings who are considered wise and intelligent, having the knowledge be given unlimited power to govern the state. He conceived that the best system of government is the government of the elites. His contention was that all people residing in the state do not possess the same and equal capacity to cultivate virtue, and therefore, all are not entitled to participate in affairs of the government. Only a few selected educational elites must be given the right to participate in the administration of the state.

Secondly, the philosopher kings who are endowed with wisdom and knowledge know, what would be the best interest of the society than the ordinary and ignorant masses. Therefore, Plato contended that the rule of philosopher king is best for the best realization of the interest of the society.

Third, according to Plato, the interest of the philosopher kings and that of the state are identical because the philosopher kings have no other interest except the welfare of the members of the community. The element of reason in philosopher king makes them to fully comprehend that the happiness of the parts depends on the happiness of whole which makes philosopher king selfless and rational, and it is the same reason that makes them to fully comprehend the best interest of the society and work for the realization of that interest.

The fourth distinct feature of Plato's philosophy of philosopher king was that it was the product of a long, rigorous and comprehensive scheme of education which lasted for 35 years beginning from birth. Since, according to him, philosopher kings were those outstanding individual of ancient Greek City-state, who successfully completed 35 years of educational training were endowed with high intellectual knowledge and wisdom, and they were fully equipped with the art of administration and ruler ship, their rule would be in the best interest of the ruled.

Finally, Plato's theory of the rule of philosophers is in unison with the socrartie conception of knowledge. To Socrates, knowledge is virtue and truth, and he who had the knowledge had virtue and truth and, he who had the knowledge never commit mistake. To Plato, knowledge makes man virtuous and wise.

Criticism

Like any other political theory, Plato's theory of the rule of philosopher kings is not free from criticisms. The follow points of criticism have been raised by different scholars of different time.

i. Plato's theory of the rule of philosopher kings gives absolute powers to the philosopher kings which leads to tyrannical system of government, and was directly against the notionof democratic system of government, which today becomes the most commonly accepted form of ideal state.

ii. Plato's theory of the rule of philosopher king was also criticized on the ground that, in such a system of government the great majority of people are to be deprived from participating in political life of the state. In other words, great injustice was being done to the great majority of the people.

iii. Plato's theory of the rule of philosopher king ignores the collective wisdom of the people and gives too much importance to the wisdom of a few philosopher kings. As a matter of fact, the collective wisdom of the greatest number of people is much superior to the collective wisdom of a few people who he calls "philosophers"

Plato, it appears, has put philosopher kings from the purview of law because he has given them complete freedom. He rejected the idea that law is the basis of state. On the other hand, he seems to put law in the background of the state. Plato, however, realized his misconception about law and makes some correction in his later writing 'The Law'.

Plato's concept of philosopher king has been criticized on the ground that it runs counter to the accepted principle of both direct and indirect democracies.

The educational curriculum Plato prescribed for philosopher kings are not sufficient to produce an efficient ruler. In his curriculum he excluded the most important and most practical subjects like law, finance and military tactics etc. which have practical administrative value.

Plato's conception that the interest of philosopher kings and that of public are identical could not be accepted. Philosopher kings are just human beings as others are, having the natural instinct of selfishness and the desire for self-preservation at the cost of others. His scheme of philosopher king would certainly lead to dictatorship of the philosopher kings.

Finally, Plato's conception of philosopher kings is a mere utopian ideal having no historical evidence of existence. It is not at all possible to have people who are totally selfless; and who could devote all their mind, body and spirit only for the furtherance of the interest of others. Therefore, his theory of philosopher king is based his wishful thinking, because philosophers mere imaginary people who make imaginary laws for imaginary commonwealth (commonwealth)

f) Plato's Concept of Ideal State

The main purpose of Plato for developing various political theories was the formation of an ideal state of his dream. With this aim in view, he has made his scheme of education of recreating philosopher kings to rule the state. He also developed his own theory of justice based on division of labor by stratifying the Greek society into three main classes based on the three elements of human soul – reason, spirit and appetite. In the same way, he also developed his own scheme of communism – communism in women and communism in property. These are the three ingredients for the establishment of an ideal state.

1. Education as the foundation or ingredient for the formation of an ideal state:

According to Plato, human mind has three elements – the element of reason, the element of spirit and the element of appetite. Based on these three elements of human soul, he divided the society into three classes; the producing class which is represented by the element of appetite of human soul, the soldier class represented by element of spirit in human soul and the ruling class represented by reason in human soul. According to him, education plays a vital role in the formation of ideal state of his dream. He advocated for compulsory education to all children, irrespective of social and economic background. His curriculum of education has been divided into three main stages and two sub-stages. The First stage beginsat the time when a child was born and lasted till a child attained the age of six. During this period, he suggested that a child must be taughtsubjects on religion and morality. The second stage begins at the age of seven and ends at the age of 18.During this period, children, he said must be trained in music which isdesigned for the positive development of human soul, and gymnastic for the development of bodyi.e. tomake the body fit. The second stage of education would make a harmonious development of body and soul. From 19 to 20 years ofage, a sub-stage would be created during which children should be given military training. This would be a compulsory military training for all. Those who could successfully completedthese two years of compulsory military training would start the next stage of educational training which he called higher education, and ends at the age of 30. During this period, the curriculum would include advance course in mathematics, which includes arithmetic, plain and solid geometry, astronomy and harmonics. There would be another test for under going further educational training for five years from 31 to 35 years of age. Those who could not go through this test would remain as soldiers whose main duty would be defence of the state from external aggression. Those who could successfully go through this test would be given educational training in dialectic or metaphysics, logic and philosophy for another five years i.e.up to 35 years.

Those who successfully completed these five years of rigorous training would be called philosopher kings; and they will be the ruler of the state for 15 years from 36 to 50 years of age. Plato's contention was that since the philosophic guardian acquired the necessary knowledge and experience, they have the wisdom and virtue and are able to rule the state in the best interest of public, for they know best what the interest of the society is. Therefore, an ideal state of his dream was the state which was ruled by the philosopher kings.

2. Justice as an ingredient of ideal state.

As discussed above, Plato classified citizens into three main groups based on professional specialization and division of labor. He said, when all the three groups of people perform their duty efficiently and effectively without getting involved in the sphere of others, there comes into existence justice, and when there is justice, there comes into existence his ideal state. When the producing classes of people represented by appetite element of human mind do their duty with utmost sincerity and dedication, production increases, and there is self-sufficiency in the supply of the necessity of life in the state. The stage, then become an ideal state. In the same way, when the soldier class of people represented by the spirit element of human mind were protecting the state and making the state safe from invasion, and were also giving security of life and property to the people,there is justice, and when there is justice there comes into being the ideal state of his dream (Plato).

Similarly, when the highest group of people, called the philosopher guardian, given maximum dedicated services to the people, there is justice and when there is justice in the state, and that state according to him, is an ideal state.

3. Communism in women and property as an ingredient of ideal state.

Plato advocated for communism in women and property for philosopher guardians. His main idea was that family and property were the root cause of evils, selfishness and greediness. Therefore, in order to prevent the guardian class from becoming selfish and greedy, Plato said, this ruling elites must be deprived of wife and property which they could claim theirs. Once they were allowed to have families of their own they would start giving more importance to their own families at the cost of the state and its interest. They will have to thinks for their wives their families and their children, and seek to maximize their welfare at the cost of that of the state. Therefore, he suggested that guardians should not have families of their own.

In the same way, he said, private property makes a man greedy and selfish. If the philosopher kings were allowed to have and maintain private properties which they could call, theirs, they would become selfish and greedy, and devote themselves for maximizing their properties as much as they could. This would lead to corruption and other evil activities detrimental to the society and state. Therefore, he wanted that guardians should be deprived of private property so that they are devoid of all evil motives. According to him, when philosopher guardians or rulers of the state do not have families of their own and private properties, properties they could claim personally belong to them, the state which they ruled over would be an ideal state, the best state of his dream.

As discussed above, Plato's theory of education, justice and communism are all complementary to each other for the establishmentof his ideal state, the best state of his dream.

Structure of Plato's Ideal State

1. ***Political Structure:*** Plato's theory of ideal state combines in it the monarchical wisdom and democratic principle of liberty and freedom. He gives much importance to obedience of law, both by the rulers and the ruled. Speaking about the importance of law, he said law and its obedience is vitally necessary for both common citizens and the philosopher kings because it enables them to have self-control and self-discipline. To quote him, 'Law is sacred and golden code of reason which is called the common law of the state" Law which he said is the product of along traditional customs and practices aims at the maximum benefit of the maximum number of people. However, he holds the view that obedience to law must be from within, that is, people should have the voluntary willingness and habit to obey law. In his second best attainable state, he said, law must be supreme and every one, both rulers and ruled are suburvient to it in the same manner and to the same degree.

Plato also, in his ideal state, created a popular assembly the membership of which was open to all citizens, a kind of direct democracy. He divides citizens in the assembly into four classes based on property in their possession. Vote in the popular assembly was determined on the basis of property in the possession of these citizens. The main function of this popular assembly was election of 37 Guardians of law and 360 members of the council. Apart from election of members of Council, the popular assembly also conducted election to the office of local officials of the city from members of the third and fourth classes. The popular assembly also elects three generals of the army on the recommendation of the guardians of law. It also suggests from time to time changes in laws of the state and decides public suites. It also decides on matter like extension of duration of residence for aliens beyond 20 years. It is, therefore, obvious that the popular assembly performs both legislative and judicial functions of today's democratic world.The Guardians of law were to be chosen from among people who were in the age group of 50 to 70 and were to hold office for 20 long years. The Guardian were expected to co-operate with the 360 members of the council in governing the state.

With regards to function, Plato assigned the council of the popular assembly purely deliberative functions. The council was divided into 12 parts, and each part was to act as the main executive organ of the government for one month. They were to act in a close coordination with the guardian of law whileperforming their duties.

2. ***Judicial System***:Regarding judicial structure and structure of organization, Plato proposed three grades of court viz. voluntary court, tribal court and court of selected judges. The voluntary courts were composing of neighbors, friends and those who were nearby, and were supposed to give best information on the nature of dispute. The tribal courts consisted of judges, selected on the basis of lots. Finally, the court of selected judges were elected from among the magistrates or guardians of law for a period of ten years. It should, however, be noted that these courts were to decide cases of private nature only,and public suits were to be decided by the popular assembly.

In addition to the political and judicial structure, Plato proposes to have a peculiar institution which he called, 'Noctoral Council' which was to consist of ten eldest members of thirty seven guardians of law. The Noctoral Council was placed outside the political structure of the state but was given the power to control and direct all legal institution. The members of this council were to be drawn from philosophers who have the perfect knowledge and wisdom who also have the knowledge of the mysteries of Heavens.

3. ***Social Structure***: With regards of social structure of Plato's ideal state,he divided citizens into four classes based on private property. The first class of people was composed of those persons whose personal property was equal to the value of their land. The second class of people consisted of those people whose property was more than the value of their land. The third class of people consisted of persons whose property was three times the value of land under their possession. The last and fourth class consisted of people whose property was four times the value of their landed property Plato insists that no one should have property the value of which is more than four times the value of his landed property. Plato insists that commodities and goods produced should be used for the common welfare of the society. Plato, therefore, while recognizing right of private property puts certain restriction on it. He puts certain upper limit i.e. four times of the value of landed property. He was not in favour of fully free economic activities, and did not also favour establishment of industry fully for the purpose of individual's benefit. Citizens, according to him, should neither keep gold and silver nor can they lend money on interest. These, he said, are for alien living in the state temporarily.

With regards to religion, he said, religious and moral principles must be the guiding principle for all citizens. But he was infamous of state control of religion and religious life of citizens. Plato was strongly against theism, because according to him, theism can assume three shapes i.e. denial of the very existence of god, denial that they are easily placated for a sin committed. He suggests for a severe punishment for the theists as they were a threat to national health for the state.

Plato's theory of ideal state has been criticized on the following grounds by different writers of different times.

First, Plato's theory of ideal state is criticized on the ground that it is highly undemocratic. In his system of ideal state, a few intellectuals who he called, Philosopher kings were given absolute power. It was against the accepted democratic principles of equality, liberty, freedom and justice (justice in modern sense of the term) There was no provision for economics, social and political equality He prescribed for the rule of a few intellectuals over much a larger section of the society for an unlimited period of time. Therefore, his theory of ideal state is unrealistic, undemocratic and untenable even in the Greek city state.

Second, Plato's contention that each element of human mind is a factor for the formation of ideal state cannot be accepted, it may be true, as he said, the state is the product of human mind but it does not necessarily mean that people residing in the state must be necessarily divided into three classes corresponding to the three elements of human mind. He suggested that in an ideal state, each class of people must perform one function only as each element of human mind preforms only each of their respective function. If his suggestion is to be followed, citizens are to be compelled to function only with a single part of his soul. The ruler must live by reason alone and has to abandon spirit and appetite. In the same way, the soldiers must live by spirit only ignoring reason and appetite. Therefore, an ideal state in which people live only with one element of their soul is an utopian ideal which is far from reality.

Third, Plato's conception that there is a continuous struggle between the element of spirit and appetite. But he said, reasons the highest element of human mind step in and established harmony between the two contending elements. In the same way, he said, there has been a continuous struggle for supremacy between soldiers and the peasants, the producing people. But people with high intellectual knowledge representing reason in human soul intervened and established harmony. This is not realistic, though logical. Since human mind does not consist of contending elements and, therefore, the sovereignty of reason does not arise. The fact of the matter is that human mind is not the home of continuously contending elements. It is a unity and it is pervaded throughout by reason.

Fifth, according to Plato's scheme of ideal state, a person would engaged in one profession throughout his life. A soldier would remain a soldier so long as he is physically capable to perform the duty of soldier. The producing members of the state would remain engaged in manual labour and the guardians would be Guardians. This scheme of water-tight division of people was doing great injustice to citizens who were expected to have a free choice of profession.

Sixth, Plato's dream of ideal state was criticized on the ground that the nature of government he proposed was against human nature. It abolished freedom of choice in selection of wife as it abolished permanent or lifelong marriage for the guardians. This arrangement was unacceptable as it was against morality and inalienable right of human being for free choice of life-partner.

Inspite of all these criticisms, Plato's theory of ideal state left deep impact on political thought in the subsequent centuries. Political thinkers, right from his time till today were much influenced by his political philosophy particularly his ideal of constitutional rules and participation of citizens in the deliberative function of state. According to Jenet"There is in the politics of Plato a utopian part and an ideal part. The first is dead and will not revive, the second is eternal."

4. Plato's contribution to Political thought:

Plato's political thought has, indeed, a tremendous influence on political thought of subsequent countries. Though Plato's concept of communism and rule of philosopher king did not have much takers on modern political thought, his works viz. statesman and law, truly left deep impact on Aristotle political philosophy and modern political thought. Plato's ideals of constitutionalism and participatory government havemuch influence on modern political liberalism. He advocated for function of state which is in conformity with the modern concept of democracy and popular government. However, maximum influence was exercise by his concept of mixed constitution as the best means for securing the stability of the government.

Some of the important political philosophy of Plato can be discussed as follows:-

1. *Concept of justice*: Plato's conception that society is always *'a unity in diversity'* and that every member of society should perform his duties to the best of his abilities and capacities deeply influence modern

political thinkers. This conception of Plato is still relevent and valid even today.

2. *Functional specialization:* Functional specialization which Plato advocates for, and which is closely related to his theory of justice, based on division of labour, is the second important contribution of Plato in the field of political thought. Functional specialization means specialized knowledge and experience, specialized knowledge and experience means efficiency and effectiveness in the areas of one's own function and duty. Efficiency and effectiveness are essential for improvement of quality of production. This results in faster economic growth which is pre-requisite for all round development.

3. *Concept of the rule of the wise and the virtuous:* Plato advocated for the rule of philosopher kings who, according to him, acquired abundant of knowledge and experience, and by virtue of which, they become wise and virtuous. Though his concept of the absolute rule of philosopher kings was not having much influence, his very conception that rulers must be well educated and well disciplined has tremendous influence on modern political thinkers.

4. *Emancipation of Women:* According to Plato, no distinction should be made between man and women in the socio economic and political life of state. He, accordingly, advocated for giving education to women on equal terms and conditions with men. This conception of Plato has a tremendous influence on modern constitutionalists who wanted to include a provision in the constitution for giving equal opportunities and status to woman in the socio economic life of the state. Even in India, it has been

seen that women are given high political posts like Presidents, Chief Minister of states and leaders of major political parties, etc.

5. *Importance given to education*:Plato insists that citizens must be given proper education and training so that they can become loyal, and dedicated citizens to the service of state. He advocated that state must provide compulsory elementary education. This conception of Plato on education has been widely accepted as the most important criterion for all round development of state. Infact educational attainment like rate of literacy, has been considered as the most reliable index of a country's economic, industrial and political development. Most of the western industrialized countries have more than 90% literacy rate as compared to below 50% literacy rate of under-developed Asia and African countries.

5. *Sense of nationalism*: Plato has given much importance to nationalism. He placed the nation above everything else. He wanted that citizens, specially, the philosopher kings, should bother for nothing else except the interest of the state. Infact, his entire philosophy was intended for promotion of national interest.

6. *First Communist*: Plato can be considered as pioneer of communist ideology. But his communism is different from modern concept of communism. He went too far for advocating communism in women and communism in property for philosopher kings. However, he is no less a communist than Karl Marx or Angels. Infact, Karl Marx and Angel borrowed much of their philosophy of communism from Plato.

7. *Father of organic theory of state:*Plato is considered as the father of organic theory of state because he is the first philosopher who make a comparison between a living organism and state. He was the first philosopher who emphasized that the state is a whole and individuals constitute the part of state.

From the fore-going discussion it is evident that Plato has left a deep and tremendous impact on subsequent political thought of subsequent countries. Importance, he has given to education, knowledge and virtue are all still occupying central idea in the political philosophy of modern world.

2

ARISTOTLE

A. Aristotle's Conception that State is a Natural Institution

According to Aristotle, state is a natural and necessary institution and that it exists for the sake of life and continues to exist for the sake of good life. Man is by nature a social animal. He cannot live alone as his needs are numerous which he alone cannot procure. For sustenance of his life he needs the accompany of others. Therefore, man and woman joint together and forms a family or household. Therefore, family is the first and earliest human institution. In the same way, a number of families'joint together and form a village community. Yet, this is not a state. Now, he said, a number of village communities together form a political society or community which is called city state. According to Aristotle the essence of state is satisfaction of human needs which is of diverse nature and which a single man could not produced. The process of social organization, therefore, is the product of an attempt to fulfill ordinary needs of man which are essential for a happy and meaningful living. State is the highest human institution which is natural and necessary and also political. The purpose of State is to provide men with necessity of life for a happy and meaningful life. In short, to Aristotle, family is the first human institution which is natural and necessary for satisfaction of basic needs of men while state is the highest, social and natural institution instituted for the fullest satisfaction of man for leading a good life.

Aristotle further said, living in a state is natural to man. Man is like other animals until he lives in a state. The will of man to live good life is a distinctive character of man which differentiates him from other animals. This very will of man culminated in the establishment of a state. Therefore, in terms of priority, he said, state is prior to man. Justifying this argument, Aristotle said, historically state comes after the existence of man, but logically the idea of state comes before the idea of man as the idea of state comes before the idea of its part. We cannot think the idea of hand or foot before thinking of a body a part of which are hands, foots etc. Hands, foot, etc. have no independent existence because once they are separated from the body they become lifeless and cannot continue to exist. In the same way, man outside the State losses his identity as a man and become animal or beast. Man, Aristotle said, is essentially political which is why he is said to be political in nature. To Aristotle, "He who does not live in a state is either a beast or a god", Man, he said, is not merely a social animal, but also political animals,because unlike other animals he strives for something higher, rather than a mere existencei.e.for a good and happy life. Other social animals like bees, elephants etc. live in groups and are social animals, but not political animals for they do not have aims and aspirations beyond mere survival or existence.

Again, Aristotle considers state as moral and natural institution. He applied the organic theory of state and maintained that the relation between individual and state was similar to that of an organism or whole. Different organs of a body perform different functions according to their different capacities and positions. In the same way, different groups of individuals in the society perform different functions according to their capacities to the best of their abilities which benefit them all. This produces a sense of responsibility, mutual regard and cooperation which strengthens their moral character. However, Aristotle maintained that some organs of a body are superior to other, so also some groups of individuals are superior to other groups of individuals. In this connection, he said, men were superior to women, free men were superior to slaves and Greeks were superior to barbarians. According to him, the relation between men and women, masters and slaves is that men were to command and women were to obey.

Explaining further the different between men and women, Aristotle maintained that women are weak of will and lack commanding capability. Her place of work is a quiet place of home and served man. As a poet said "Silence is a woman glory" woman is at best when she is silently obeying. The will of man, Aristotle accordingly, denied women from the right of citizenship.

The foregoing discussion on Aristotle's conception of state as a natural Institution clearly makes us to believe that state was created purely for the satisfaction of the diverse needs of man. He maintained that state is the highest human institution which is politically, socially and economically necessary for continuous existence and for realization of good and happy life which man is seeking.

Aristotle's Theory of Ideal State

A close examination of Aristotle's concept of state leads us to understand that state, according to him, has the following features.

First, Aristotle's ideal state is a small city state, small both in terms of population and territory. People in such a state consists of citizens whose social life overshadowed the interest of family, religion and friendly personal relationship.

Second, Aristotle gives an important dominant position to law in his ideal state. He was totally against the despotic and dictatorial rule of a few intellectuals, how virtuous and wise they might be, instead, he was infavour of the impartial and impersonal rule of law, because, he said, law represents the wisdom of community since time immemorial. Therefore, law is supreme and everyone in the state is subordinated to it.

Third, it appears that Aristotle considers state as an ethical institution. The reason, he said, was state aims at the moral improvement of citizens. According to him, individual can achieve his highest moral and intellectual development through and by membership of state. The ideal state of Aristotle, therefore, aims at promotion of a good and a happy life by which he means a virtuous and moral life.

Fourth, education plays a prominent role in the ideal state of Aristotle, because education is instrumental in making virtuous citizens. He was in favour of state control of education. He suggested that state should regulate education and make it compulsory for all citizens so that citizens could cultivate good habits to become a perfect citizen. Perfection, he said, could be achieved only by cultivating a moral and intellectual excellence which is possible only through a system of uniform compulsory public education. But it should be noted that his scheme of education was meant only for citizens and not for slaves, alien and women.

Fifth, as against Plato's concept of ideal state which rejected the institution of private property for guardian class, Aristotle maintained that private property is a natural institution which must be preserved and protected. He suggested for equal distribution of land to citizens. With regards to property other than land, he said, the value of property an individual possessed should be decided on the basis of his landed property. The value of property that an individual possessed should not exceed four times the value of his landed property. He said that the product of the land should be distributed among the people and should be used for common welfare of the public.

Sixth, Aristotle applied the principle of division of labour in his ideal state. He assigned agricultural activities to slaves, trade and industry to resident aliens and political function to citizens. Division of labour was based on division of people according to their natural capacity and educational standard and experience.

Seventh, with regards to the size of territory and population, Aristotle did not prescribe a specific size, but maintained that the population and territory should not be too small or nor too large but must be of manageable size.

Eight, an ideal state, according to him, (Aristotle) must be self-sufficient and should not have aggressive designed against other foreign countries. The state should fully concentrate for the fullest mental, moral and economic development of men.

Ninth, ideal state of Aristotle was dominated by middle class. He believes that only middle class could provide stability to state because middle class could strike a balance between the conflicting claims of the rich and the poor. To quote him "The addition of a large number of middle class has a greatly influence and checks the opposite extremes" He opines that the total number of middle class should outnumber the collective number of both the rich and the poor. Then only an ideal state could be established.

Tenth, an ideal state should have easy access to sea for easy transportation of imports and exports. However, he said, state should not be too close to sea, otherwise,there could be a problem with defence.

Finally, Aristotle's ideal system appears to be having aristocracy as the form of government. He does not specifically mention the form or system of government in his deal state, but since he was in favour of the rule of middle class, it seems that he favours aristocracy as the best form of government which he believes could bring about stability and all-round development of citizens.

Aristotle's Conception that State is the Highest and Supreme Association

Aristotle considers state as a supreme and highest human association. While other associations aims at some good, the State " embraces all the rest, and aims in a greater degree than any other , the highest good", The State, according to him, is the culmination of social evolution and also because man realizes his highest moral perfection in and through the membership of state. Family and village exist essentially for the preservation of life and the comfort of companionship, but the state exists for the sake of good life and not only for the sake of life, and political society exists for the sake of noble actions and not for mere partnership looking from the point of view of man's own nature as state is the highest form of association. According to Aristotle, in the family man reproduces himself, in the village, he satisfies his elementary needs of companionship, but in the state man realizes his entire self, and particularly the highest self as an association of men for the sake of best moral life.

It is, therefore, evident from the above discussion that state is the supreme and the highest form of human association, because the aims of the state is higher and nobler than the aims of other associations. The state aims at the highest good of all including moral perfection.

Functions of Aristotle's Ideal State

The main aim of state, according to Aristotle was realization of a perfect and self-sufficing life, by which he meant a happy and honorable life. With this aim in view, the state he said, must create essential conditions for mental, moral and physical development of the people. He did not want to restrict the function of state to mere preservation of the rights of its members. The function of state must be promotion of the good. The state must provide education to the members of state for enabling them to perform each of their function effectively and efficiently with much dedication and with sense of duty. The State should train citizen to live a righteous life.

In short, according to Aristotle, the primary objectively and function of state is to make citizens righteous and moral.

B. Aristotle's Conception of Justice

Aristotle's theory of justice constitutes an important part of his political philosophy, but his conception of justice is quite different from Plato's and other Greek philosopher's conception of justice. Aristotle developed his own theory of justice which are of two types.

The Universal or complete justice, he said, was a moral virtue concerned with regulation of public and social relation. The universal justice, in other words, means obedience to law and could be realized only in an ideal state. Particular justice, according to Aristotle, on the other hand was related to distribution of public offices and observance of the rule of proportionate equality. In other words, particular justice has to do something with distribution of wealth, honour and goods proportionately.

Aristotle further classified particular justice into two more groups viz. distributive justice and corrective justice. Distributive justice, according to him, implies proportionate allocation of public office according to the worth of individual, and was concerned primarily with political privilege. Distributive justice, according to him, is the most important instrument for prevention of revolution. Distributive justice ensures that every individual gets his due share as a member of the society and keeps him satisfied with what he received.When every individual is made satisfied and contented, he would not join any revolutionary movement for over throwing of the existing government. Therefore, distribution justice is the best weapon in the hands of the rulers to prevent revolution. Aristotle was, however in favour of allocation public offices to the virtuous only, because he believes that the virtuous could make best contribution to the society. He was against the allocation of public offices to ignorant citizens who lack sufficient knowledge to run public office. This implies denial of public offices to great majority of citizens, because virtuous are few in number and would mean superficial inequality. But Aristotle holds the view that this would be true distributive justice, because to give such important public offices to non-virtuous and ignorant masses would be unjust or injustice being done to the society.

Distributive justice, is based on the principle of proportionate equality. For e.g.Mr. A and Mr. B made some contribution to promote the general welfare of the society, they were supposed to receive office of honour from the state. If the two made the same contributing to the society, they ought to be given the same reward or equal reward. But if Mr. A's contribution is more than that of Mr.B's, then Mr. A. ought to be given more rewards than Mr. B. This is what Aristotle calls "Distribution justice based on proportionate allocation of public office"

With reference to corrective justice Aristotle said, it was essentially negative in character and was concerned with commercial transection. The main aim of corrective justice is, to restore or give back to each person what he had lost. Corrective justice, he said, relates to voluntary and commercial transactions like heir, sale and furnishing of security etc. and with involuntary action involving aggression on life, property, honour and freedom. In other words, corrective justice means to free individual from unlawful confiscation of his property and to free him from unlawful threat to his life. This implies that state has to provide security of life and property to citizens.

C. Theory of CITIZENSHIP

Aristotle in his Book III of Politics discussed as who is a citizens and who is not. He holds the view that all residents of a state are not citizens. With regards to citizenship he was a conservative Greek political thinker because he wanted to conserve and maintain the then existing institution of citizenship. In ancient Greek City State of Athen, citizenship was conferred to those privileged class of people who held public offices and participate in the state activities', and functions.

While explaining his concept of citizenship, Aristotle said, mere resident of a state is not a citizens. He held that slaves and residents aliens also reside in a state, but they are not citizens. In the same way, enjoyment of legal rights like right to sue and to be sued does not make a person to become citizen because such rights can also be given to aliens and slaves who are not consider citizen. Again, according to him, a person cannot be a citizen simply because his father or fore father was a citizen.

Then, who are to be conferred the right of citizenship? According to Aristotle, only those people in a state who participated in the administration of justice and legislation as member of deliberative assembly were included as citizens of a state. In other words, only a person holding office of judge and member of popular assembly is a citizen.There are also other three essential, but not absolute, however, conditions for conferment of citizenship which are as follows.

In the first place, a citizen must be a resident of the state, he must have enjoyed legal rights like right to sue and to be suied in court of law, he must be a descent from citizen i.e. his father or fore-father must have been citizens. Again, to be a citizen, one must have the capacity to rule and be ruled. He went a step further and said, a citizen or to become a citizen, one must have sufficient leisure because, leisure is essential for cultivating virtue and for devoting one's whole to the service of state. He also insists that in order to have citizenship right, a person must have sufficient property to support his family so that he is not engaged in manual labour to support family. He, at the same time, insists that a citizen must be one who has slaves. His idea was that, a person who has to engaged himself in manual labour to earn his necessities of life cannot be an effective citizen. Slaves, therefore, would be a necessity for production of necessities of life so that the master who is considered citizen would be in a better position to spend maximum of his time for the service of state.

With regard to the question that what is virtue which is essential for conferment of citizenship. Aristotle compares it with a sailor. He said, all those who work in a ship are all sailors, but they perform different function. One of them is a rower and other is a pilot, and the third one is a lockout. Every one of them has a virtue of his own, different from one another, but they all have common objectives i.e. the safety of navigation. In the same way, citizens he said, may differ from one another and they may perform different functions according to their capacities and areas of specialization, yet they have one common objective i.e. to serve the state and protect and further the interest of the society. This is what Aristotle calls, the first virtue of citizens.

There is another question i.e. what is the difference between citizens and rulers. The main distinction between the two, Aristotle said, was the ruler has a practical wisdom while citizens have the right and true opinion without real practical wisdom.

There is another pertinent question i.e. who are not a citizens? Answering this question, Aristotle said slaves, resident aliens, foreigner, mechanics, labourer and all others resident engaged in manual labour are to be denied of citizenship right, because these peoples are engaged in fulltime manual labour and have no sufficient time to fully devote themselves to the service of the state. He further said that, women, children and aged people must not be confered citizenship right. According to him, women are born inferior to men and, therefore, lack intellectual capacity; children, he said should also be denied of citizenship right, because they are not having maturity of judgment to take part in the affairs of the state. Likewise, he also excluded old and sick people from the category of citizens, because they are physically not fit to perform the function of state effectively.

With regards to a question i.e. what is the function of citizens? Aristotle said that, the main function of citizens is to be in the service of state, to engage his whole being, time and energy, capacity and ability to the service of the community for the common good of all. He has to be selfless and have sufficient will to do his best for the community.

Who are then, According to Aristotle, Included in the Category of Citizens?

(Qualification for citizenship)

1. Descendants of citizens i.e. persons whose parents or grant parents are citizens.
2. People who are endowed with virtue
3. People who have sufficient leisure
4. People who have property and slaves
5. Must be having legal right to sue and to be sued
6. Must have the capacity to rule and be ruled

The following categories of people are denied of citizenship by Aristotle.

1. Slaves
2. Resident-aliens
3. Foreigners
4. Mechanics
5. Children

6. Women
7. Old and aged people
8. Manual labourers

Criticisms of Aristotle's theory of Citizenship:

The following points of criticism are put up by different writers on Aristotle theory of citizenship:

1. Aristotle's conception that women, children and old aged people should be excluded from citizens could not be accepted. Women, children, aged people who constitute a very large section of the society could not be excluded from citizenship right as they are also sons of the soil like any other who Aristotle called citizen. It would be a complete injustice to deny them of citizenship right.
2. Laborers and other manual workers constitute a very important and useful part of the state. It is they who produce necessities of life and make other class of people to have leisure. Their services are so important for the sustenance of life that without them the state cannot just exist and function. Therefore, the exclusion of these groups of people from citizenship right is not acceptable in any given society or state.
3. Aristotle gives too much importance to property. He asserts that only propertied class of people could become citizens and act as legislators or jurors.This naturally gives rise to middle class-government and ignored a large section of people who belong to working class.

4. Aristotle was doing great injustice to people who do not have leisure by denying them political rights and right to education. The working classes are made as mere instrument of leisured class people.
5. Aristotle has made a sharp division of society into two main classes- the working and producing class and the leisured class who he has given them political right. This kind of division of people into citizens and non-citizens would do more harm than good for the society and state as it would result in mistrust, disloyalty and disunity among different sections of society in the state. It can even lead to revolution for overthrowing the existing government or it can be a destabilizing and dis-integrating factor which can cause the total extinction of the State.
6. Aristotle's conception of citizenship is not in conformity with modern conception of citizenship. In modern state citizenship is not based on property or nature of work. Whether a person is rich or poor or whether a person is working in factory or is engaged as manuallaborer he is not denied of citizenship right
7. Aristotle's scheme of direct participation of all citizens in the legislative and judicial function of state is neither possible nor practicable in modern large state.
8. Aristotle's conception of citizenship is not in conformity with the organics theory of state.

In spite of all these criticisms, Aristotle cannot be totally blamed for developing his theory of citizenship. His concept of citizenship was particularly meant for

Greek City State which had a very small population. In such city-state, participation of citizens in the affairs of the state was possible.

Therefore, his theory of citizenship has some relevance in Greek City-State.

D. Aristotle's Theory of Slavery

"Since some men are slaves by nature, and others are free men, it is clear that where slavery is advantageous to any one, then it is just to make them slave"

Aristotle considers the institution of slavery as a natural institution. He said some men are by nature slaves, and some men are free men. And those slaves are slaves not only in the interest of their master, but also in their own interest. He considers slaves as the living possession of family and they are the living property of their masters. His point was that though slave has the mental power to understand and physical power to follow reason, he has no sufficient reasoning power. Therefore, Aristotle said, slaves are at their best when they obey the order of their masters who are endowed with more and higher capacities.

In reply to a question, who is a slave? Aristotle said, anyone who is by nature not his own man but an other's is a slave. By saying this, he means to say a person who has no personality and mind of his own, is a slave... Slavery, he said, is a natural institution, it embodies the principle of subordination of the rule by the superior over the inferiors. It is in accordance with this principle that the soul rules over the body and it is much beneficial and better for the body that it is ruled over by the soul. In the same way, it is natural and better for the soul to be ruled over by mind. This principle also applied in relation between man and animal as it is better for animals when they are ruled over by man. Also this principle of relationship is applicable between man and woman. It is better for woman to be ruled over by man, because man has more physical and mental capacities than woman. According to Aristotle, this general principle is applicable to all human beings, and that all those human beings who have no capacity to develop themselves are slaves by nature. It is better for these people to be slaves than be free men.

Reasons for Justification of the Institution of Slavery

There are three main reasons why Aristotle justified the institution of slavery such as natural, necessity and expediency.

i. *Natural*: Rejecting the view of radical sophists who said that men are by birth equal, Aristotle said, men are not born equals. He maintained that nature has made men unequal as nature itself endowed men with different qualities and capacities and ordained that, the superior men should rule over the inferiors.

   Being naturally inferiors, some men have to accept their inferior capacities and surrender to the service of those naturally superiors. This is not only in the interest of their masters and the community, but also is in the interest of themselves. This is the law of nature. Explaining the natural relationship between slaves and master, Aristotle said, it is as impossible for a householder to live a good life without slaves as it is impossible for musicians to produce good musics without musical instrument

ii. *Necessity:* Slave, according to Aristotle is a necessity in the larger interest of thecommunity. He said that masters should be free from material worries so that they may be in a better position to serve the community. It is here that the slaves become a necessity to provide the masters with free time to concentrate themselves fully in the affairs of public. This is in the larger interest of the community as a whole. The slaves, he said, are able to attain their best when they serve their master according to their advice. Therefore, the institution of slavery becomes a necessary and useful institution.

iii. *Expediency:* Aristotle also justifies slavery on the ground of expediency. During his contemporary Greek, slaves played very important role in the maintenance and operation of green economy. The major portion of people living in city-state depends much on slaves for material needs and the absence of slave would have much impact, adversely, of course, on the social fabric of the city-sate. Slaves are the animate property of citizens who provide with materials conditions necessary for sustenance. Therefore, for the purpose of expediency, Aristotle said, slaves are inevitable.

Who are to be Enslaved and who are not to be Enslaved, According to Aristotle?

Answering this question, Aristotle said, everybody or anybody cannot be enslaved. He approved slavery only on certain conditions. Only those persons who are mentally deficient should be enslaved and prisoners of war should not be enslaved under any circumstances. The reason he said was, victory in war did not necessarily mean intellectual superiority of the victor or the mental deficiency of the vanquished.Therefore, Aristotle did not want enslavement of prisoners of war.

Again, Aristotle insisted that master should give humanely treatment to their slaves and suggested that the state should give punishment to those masters who ill-treated their slaves.

Finally, Aristotle said that there must be emancipation of slaves who showed good conduct and developed their capacity for reasoning and virtue.

Criticisms of Aristotle's Theory of Slavery

Aristotle's concept of slavery is subjected to a number of criticisms of which the following could be mentioned.

First, Aristotle's conception that men are born unequal is against the modern notion of equality that men are born equal. His conception that some men are born to rule and some others are born to be ruled is against the modern concept of equal opportunity to all i.e. equal opportunities to be ruler as well as to be ruled over.

Second, Aristotle's theory of slavery is based on the notion that Greeks are superior race and they should be the rulers. But this conception was considered devoid of truth because there was no such thing as racially superior as men are born equal. This means men, whether Greeks or barbarians, black or white, yellow or brown are all born equal.

Third, Aristotle considers slavery as a hereditary institution and therefore, said that some men are slave by nature. But he does not lay down any criteria for determining as to who is a natural slave and who is not. Modern writers hold the view that environment is a more important factor for slavery than hereditary.

Fourth, Aristotle's theory of slavery is contradicting his own theory of human nature. He said on one occasion that man is by nature good and finds his perfection in the society. On the other occasion, he again subjected a numerically larger group of people to be in a perpetual enslavement without any hope of emancipation. Therefore, Aristotle is contradicting himself.

Finally, Aristotle's theory of slavery is against the notion of social justice. On the one hand, Aristotle puts much emphasis on the important contribution of state to the society, but on the other hand he does not give any criteria nor does he provide, any reward in return to their services. This is clear violation of the concept of social justice.

E. Aristotle's Theory of Revolution

Aristotle, in his book V of Politics, discussed his theory of revolution. There were frequent changes in the government of Greek City-State, and to find out the causes of these changes in the government, Aristotle made extensive study of the working of 158 constitutions of Greek city states. After studying the working of these constitutions, he developed his theory of revolution in which he has given his own meaning of revolution, its causes and offered his own measures for prevention of revolution in Greek city-states.

Regarding the meaning of revolution, Aristotle said, revolution has two meanings. First, it means a major or minor change in the constitution like change from monarchy to oligarchy and so on. Second, it means a change in the ruling power without a change in the constitution that is, change in the form of government, or a change in the people who hold the powers of the government. It may also be interpreted as a change in the social and political system as a whole.

Causes of Revolution

Aristotle, after studying and analyzing the revolutionary conditions of Greek City-States classified the causes of revolution into two broad categories which are discussed as follows:-

1. General Causes

According to Aristotle, people have the natural desire to be treated equally. When people see other people being treated superior to other, they have the natural desire to overthrow them from their existing superior position by changing the social and political set up. For this, people who are treated inferior normally, have the will to resort to revolution for overthrowing the existing governmental people in power. According to Sinclair, since justice and friendship are the moral basis of the state, injustice and ill-will are the most potent causes of discontentment and instability. The absence of proportionate equality of a fair deal leads to lack of justice and splits the city into factions. There can be no fellow feeling when one section of the community is convinced that its rights are being denied to it and justice is not being done'

Therefore, According to Aristotle, revolution for change in the government or political system takes place when a substantial section of people in the state feels that justice is not being done to them. Aristotle drew a close link between stability and equality.

II. Particular causes of revolution

According to Aristotle, the followings are indirectly the particular causes or factors provoking political revolution for change in the constitution or government or change of power holders.

1. *Social, political and economic inequality.*

   When there exists in the state social, political and economic inequality, those who are treated unequal or inferiors who forms a larger section of the society, demand for equality in those fields in which they are unequal. This leads to revolution for change of the system which may ultimately result in the change of the whole political system including the power structure, system of government etc.

2. *Giving of undue privileges to a few selected people.*

   Giving undue importance and priviledge, to a few selected people makes a much larger section of people to develop a feeling that they are being denied of those privileges, and start mobilizing public opinion which may be a serious threat to the unity and solidarity of the state leading to revolution.

3. *Giving absolute power to a few individuals.*

   Giving absolute and unlimited powers to single person or a few individuals is bound to be resented by those who are deprived of the same. This leads to tyranny of a few against the vast majority which ultimately provoke revolution.

4. *Misuse of power by the authority.*

   When the authority of state adopted an attitude of aggressive nature against the opponents, it is resented to by the opponents and start revolution to overthrow the authority.

5. *Disproportionate increase of any part of state-territories social etc.*

   The disproportionate increase of a part of the state is also another cause of revolution. The proletariat revolutions are mainly due to disproportionate increase in the strength of the poor and the absence of a strong middle class.

6. *Attempt of wrong-doer to conceal their wrong deeds*

   Attempt of wrong-doors among the ruling elites to conceal their wrong deeds when exposed are much resented to by the people leading to revolution. In other words, concealment of misdeeds by authority is likely to cause revolution as and when their misdeeds are finally exposed.

7. *Election intrigue.*

   The practice of unfair election by the authority to capture political power is much resented to by the people, and that they may resort to revolution at an opportune time.

8. *Recruitment of disloyal citizen to public office.*

   Appointment of disloyal citizens to the post of public offices may generate revolution.

9. *Diversity of culture and people.*

   When the population of state consists of diverse groups of people, speaking diverse languages and having diverse cultures, there is a high possibility of irreconcilable disagreements on various issues which may ultimately lead to revolution.

10. *Excessive use of force.*

    Excessive use of force by the authority may lead to revolution as and when people lost patience and tolerance. People may for sometimes, could tolerate, but if the authority continues to adopt such excessive force crossing the limit of people's tolerance, people could start to retaliate the authority by starting a revolution.

11. *Neglect of minor changes.*

    Like a neglected spark may cause wild fire, neglect of minor change may also lead to revolution. An incident or a change in the system which appears to be minor if not given timely check, it may in the long run cause or lead to full-scale revolution.

12. *Free flow of immigrants.*

    Immigrants, who are having different social, political, economic and justice system may bring into existence revolution for change of political, social and economic system of their host state.

13. *Conquered nation and state.*

    The conquest of a foreign state also contains seeds of revolution. People of the invaded state are always looking for opportunity to retaliate the conqueror, and when the opportune time comes, would strike back in the form of revolution or otherwise. The threat could become more serious if the conqueror adopts aggressive policy towards the nationals of the sub nation.

III. Causes of revolution in different forms of government

Aristotle finlay has given the causes of revolution in different forms of government. According to him, in Democracies, revolutions are usually the outcome of excessive use of power and unwarranted condemnation of the rich by the demagogues. In Oligarchies, he said, revolutions are caused by rivalry and dissensions among the oligarchs or they may be caused by the oppressive rule of the ruling oligarchs. In Aristocracy, revolutions are caused by denial of honour to much a larger section of people. In other words, in aristocracy, revolutions are caused by monopoly of honour by a few aristocrats.

In polity, Aristotle said, revolutions are generated by defective balance of different elements in the constitution. In monarchy and tyranny, he said, revolution are caused by two factors viz. hatred and contempt in the mind of the people because of oppressive and dictatorial nature of the rule of the monarchs and tyrants.

Preventive Measures

Aristotle, after explaining the most common causes of revolution has given preventive measures for avoiding revolution in different forms of government which could be broadly discussed under the following two heads:-

1. General Preventive measures

In the first place, Aristotle said, efforts should be made by the rulers to win over the confidence of all sections of people by removing all kinds of injustice and treat all classes of people equally and give equal consideration. Public offices should be open to all based on merit and not be treated as the monopoly of any particular class of people.

In the second place, the rulers must educate the people about the importance and necessity of obedience to law, and make them law abiding citizens. With this aims in view, even a minor breach of minor law should be viewed seriously by the ruler.

In the third place, citizens must be given sufficient knowledge of the constitution. Once citizens, slaves and resident – aliens are well verse in the working of the constitution, they would learn by themselves how to adapt themselves with the functioning of the government, and there would be a little possibility of revolution. Aristotle considers imparting of education to people on the working of constitution as the surest preventive measure for avoiding revolution, and for ensuring the stability of the government.

In the fourth place, Aristotle said that even a minor change in the state should be viewed seriously and attended promptly because negligence of such minor change may ultimately result in total revolution.

In the fifth place, Aristotle said that as a preventive measure to revolution, no individual or group of individuals should even be given too much power. This would certainly be resented to by majority of people who are denied of such power. This, in due course may generate revolution to remove those who are in power.

In the sixth place, efforts should be made so that public offices free of corruption and to ensure this, efforts should be made to check bribery and other illegal activities in public offices. He even suggested that all public offices should be made honorary.

In the seventh place, no public servant should be allowed to occupy public office on permanent basis. Aristotle was holding the opinion that if a public office bearer is allowed to occupy public office permanently, he may tend to behave in a manner detrimental to the interest of the state and may lead to a revolt by the people.

In the eight place, Aristotle holds the view that as far as practicable there should be no sudden and unexpected promotion to political post; in case promotion is at all to be made, it should be gradual and out of necessity. Sudden and quick promotion is likely to be resented by the people which may lead to revolution.

In the ninth place, important public offices should not be occupied by resident-alien or foreigner because an outsider who is not a citizen cannot be expected to have much concern for the welfare of the state as natives do, for they lack loyalty to the state.

In the tenth place, every effort should be made to make citizens patriotic, and this spirit of patriotism should be maintained by the people. For this, people should be made to feel that the state is their own. A watchful eye should always be put on the movement and behavior of the people, and see that people have full loyalty to the state.

In the eleventh place, public offices should be distributed among the people as wide and inclusive as possible. No one should develop a feeling that public offices are meant solely for him and that he has to be made aware that recruitment to such public offices are made on the basis of merit only.

Lastly, the details of administration, particularly those of public finance should be open to public scrutiny. In other words, details of administration, particularly those related to public finance should be transparent and people should be made to feel that public servants are actually working without selfish motive. If people are kept in dark about what is going on in public offices they may develop a suspicious feeling that they are being exploited and may revolt against them.

2. Particular Preventive Measures

Aristotle after giving general preventive measures for prevention of revolution, gives particular measures to be adopted in different forms of government. In democracy, he suggested that the rich should be made to feel that their properties and estates are not their sole personally property, but they are the properties of common people to be used for common good and benefits. In Aristocry and oligarchy,peoples should be treated with fairness and that no single individual or group of individuals should be made too powerful. Poor and ordinary people should also be given opportunity to participate in administration of state. In polity, revolution could be avoided by proper blending of the positive democratic and oligarchic elements.

In tyranny, Aristotle suggested the following preventive measures for avoiding revolution.

Having good espionage system including women spies.

Making people to feel that the state is in constant danger of external treat from powerful enemy.

To adopt a policy of aggression and expansion.

To develop the intellectual capacity of citizens.

To keep people poor so that they may not have time to participate in political activities.

To create a sense of hostility among the people so that they are busy among themselves.

To make people religious and make them to spread much of their off-times in public worship and religious ceremonies.

To make people to earn reputation for military virtue.

To show favours personally, but punish them through third party.

To chop off heads of inconvenient rulers.

From the above discussed causes and preventive measures suggested by Aristotle, it is undoubtedly evident that Aristotle has a clear and deep understanding of human mind. Many of the causes and preventive measures he has given are not altogether out-dated even today. Infact, they are still revelvent in the modern democratic political system and his contribution could not be neglected by modern political thinkers.

Aristotle's view on the best attainable state

Aristotle, after discussing his theory of ideal state admitted that most of his idealstate are in the true sense, unattainable or practicable. Therefore, he has given a detailed account of the best attainable state. This best attainable state avoids the extremes of democracy and oligarchy. This, Aristotle calls, constitutional Government or polity.

Aristotle uses the terms 'Polity' in two different senses – General and particular. In the general sense, the term 'Polity' according to Aristotle, means constituting whether it be monarchy, aristocracy, oligarchy or democracy. In the particular sense, he wanted the fusion between democratic and oligarchic elements, while avoiding their extreme elements. According to Aristotle, in oligarchy a few rich persons ruled over a much larger poor people for protection of their class interests. The main qualification of holding public offices in such a system is ownership of property i.e. richness. The interest of the ruling class in such a system is only protection andpromotion of their class interests i.e. their property. In the process they adopted aggressive rule over the poor. In democracy the poors, by virtue of their number dominate the affairs of the state. The best attainable state, according to him, is a balance between extreme richness and extreme poverty. The ultimate best attainable state, therefore, is the rule of middle class who are not too poor nor too rich, either. He called such state as polity. This is what he called the best attainable state. He suggested that the middle class must constitute the largest group, larger than the poor and the rich together.

Therefore, Aristotle's best attainable ideal state is the state ruled by the middle classes as the middle class strikes a balance between democracy dominated by the poor and oligarchy dominated by a few rich.

3

MACHEAVELLI

A. Separation of politics from ethic and religion

Machiavelli made a clear and deliberate separation of politics from ethics and religion. He holds the opinion that for the attainment of political objective, the prince must resort to any means, whether moral or immoral, ethical or unethical because in politics the ends justified the means. He even permitted the prince to use immoral and unethical means like fraud, forgery trickery, breach of faith and contract, violence, etc. So long as the end is maintenance of the unity and integrity of the state, the prince has to resort to all means without moral and ethical consideration. To quote him "Let the prince, then look to the maintenance of the state, the means will always be deemed honorable and will receive general approbation." In other words, his quotation could be interpreted to mean that so long as the purpose is the maintenance of state, any means, whether moral or immoral, ethical or unethical would be welcomed by the general public.

Machiavelli maintained that the state has reasons and that reasons of state are superior to the principles of morality. The reason of state, he said, justified the adoption of any means including treachery and brutality. In his famous work 'Discourse', he writes, 'When the safety of our country is absolutely at stake there need be no questions of what is just or unjust, merciful or cruel, praise-worthy or disgraceful but all the considerations set a side, that course alone is to be taken which may save our country and maintain its liberty" The main focus of Machiavelli, therefore, is the security and safety of the state, and nothing else, even moral and ethical consideration should be a hindrance to the activities of state for ensuring the unity and security of state.

Mecheavelli also maintained that individual should not be allowed to practice morality of politics in private life. He was against the murder of breach of faith among the individuals in the society, because such act would certainly infringe upon the life and security of other fellow members of the society. Individual, Mecheavelli said, should act in an upright manner. On the other hand, Mecheavelli maintained that state should not be necessarily constrained by moral and ethical principles so long as the purpose is the furtherance of the interest of the state.

Though Mecheavelli hold the view that the prince should not be constrained by moral principle in the interest of the state, he also at the same time suggested that the prince should appear to be an embodiment of qualities which are highly esteemed. He should behave as if he is an embodiment of mercy, good faith, integrity, kindliness and religious. Therefore, while he considers force as the prime factor for the regulation of the affairs of the state, he also puts focus on the importance of religion and wanted the church to be an instrument for creating national customs and habits of thought which will help in maintaining peace and order in the society. This means that Mechiavelli wanted the church to be an instrument for the achievement of political goals.

From the above discussed conception of separation of politics from morality and ethics put forward by Mechiavelli, it is evident that Mechiavelli proposed two different types of morality-one for the ruler and the other for the citizens. The ruler is outside the purview of morality of individuals as he has a separate morality. The prince or the ruler is not bound by the morality of other group of individuals as he is not within the group. The ruler who is also the creator of state is not only outside the law, but he enacts morality and decides what is moral and what is immoral, he is outside morality as well. There is no authority to judge his acts except the success of political expedients of perpetuating his state.

While Mechiavelli was severely condemned for advocating openly immorality in public life, a close analysis of his view will make us to believe that he is neither moral nor immoral, but unmoral rather. As Prof. Maxey said "in Mechiavelli's eye the state knows no ethics. What it does is neither ethical nor unethical. It is of neutral gender so far as right and wrong are concerned".

Criticism.

Mechiavelli's theory of separation of politics from morality, religion and ethic has been criticized on the follow points:-

In the first place, Mechiavelli seems to give free hands to politician to commit crimes of all sorts on the pretext of protecting the unity and integrity of the state.

In the second place, he seems to have the understanding that the interest of the rulers and that of the public is always in uniformity which is not always true. There is no permanent rule which could determine the interest of the state and that, the ruler could always act in his personal selfish interest in the name of the interest of state.

Man, who he said are selfish, wicked, degenerate, and opportunist are with all certainty, shall act to suit their selfish interest, and that the ruler who is also just human being could be motivated by his selfish interest to act with the aims to achieve his selfish objective which is against the interest of the state. Therefore, Mecheavelli'sconception of separation of politics from morality and ethics is against his own theory of human nature.

B. Influence and Contribution of Macheavelli to political thought

Though there are, like any other thinkers a number of shortcomings, contradictions and deficiencies in the Machiavelli's political philosophy, particularly, his giving of absolute power to the prince and princes, his political thought certainly constitutes an important development in the history of modern political thought. The under discussed point are some of the most important contributions he has made for the development of modern political thought.

He is, perhaps, the first political thinker to reject the feudal conception of hierarchical autonomous entities and introduced the conception of territorial, national and sovereign state which enjoyed supreme power over citizens and subjects, and over all other institutions in the state.

He is the first thinkers to free politics from ethics and religion. He, for the first time maintained that there were two distinct standards of morality – the morality of the state and morality of individuals. By making a distinction between these two moralities, he freed the state from the liability of moral principles. Most political thinkers of today are endorsing his separation of morality and ethic for the state and individual because the same standard of morality, ethic and religion could not be applied to state and individuals at the same degree.

Macheavelli was the first thinker to denounce the authority of the church over the state. He was the first thinker to maintain that the church should be subordinated to the state.

Mecheavelli was the first thinker who contributed the idea of materialism to political philosophy. He has given materialistic interpretation of the origin of state, and rejected the metaphysical and supernatural elements in the emergence and development of state. Though his materialistic interpretation of the origin of state is not fully identical with Karl Marx's concepts of the same, it does tremendously influence Karl Marx in developing his theory of the origin of state.

He was the first political thinker to advocate the principle of power politics. He maintained that the state should either expand or perish which means state should strive by all possible means to increase its power or if it cannot it should extinct or perish rather than incapable of expanding its power.

Macheavelli's development of historical method has proved to be agreat contribution to the development of modern political thought.

He was also a pragmatic thinker whose conception on politics, religion, ethics and morality are practical or pragmatic philosoply.

Lastly, the knowledge of human psychology, which he advised the prince to possess, is his valuable contribution.

When the rulers are fully conscious of the minds and aspiration of the people, they would be able to rule in the interest of the people and will make them popular consequently.

Conclusion

The contribution of Mecheavelli to the development of modern political thought is so great that he is referred to as the father of modern political thought. He is the pioneer of modern political thinker to separate the authority of the church from that of the state, and it is he who made the church subordinated to the state for the first time in the history political thought.

"And in the action of men and specially the princes, from which there is no appeal, the end justifies the means"

Explain the underlining meaning of the above statement of Mechiavelli.

Mercheavelli, by giving the statement means to say that so long as the ends or goal is to secure the security, safely, stability and growth of the power of the state, the prince or ruler could adopt any means, because the end is considered sound. Mecheavelli, as a matter of fact, devoted his entire political philosophy towards the promotion of the interest of the state. He calls any end as sound and good if that end is the protection of state and its authority.

With the aim to achieve the interest of the state, the prince, he said, must not hesitate to use any method, how repressive or forceful it night be. Mecheavelli event advised the prince to adopt extreme form of punishment to his political opponents and said, he should right away execute his opponents instead of giving other form of punishments like confiscation of their property.

Therefore, the main underlining idea of the above statement is that the ruler or the prince is the creator of state itself and the law there-within endowed with sovereign and absolute power over citizens and subjects, unrestrained by law. Therefore, any means adopted by the ruler or prince for the security and safety of the state is justified. It is because of this he said "the ends justified the means"

C. JEAN BODIN

Bodin's Conception of State:

Jean Bodin traces the origin of state to the natural social instinct of man. Man, being a social animal, could not live an isolated and a solitary life. He has an inborn instinct to live in groups. The state, therefore, Bodin said, is the product of the social instinct of man. The social instinct of man brought man out of family life and gave birth to statehood. It was also the social instinct of man which gave birth to other social institution which eventually gave birth to a political institution. This according to Bodin, was the origin of state.

State, according to Bodin, was an association of associations including family. He maintained that state is the highest form of human associations because sovereignty was vested in it which, other associations were deprived of. It is the state which has the power to rule over all other associations and regulates their functioning and operations. Bodin maintains that state has a soul as well as the body which is in conformity with the organic theory of state Bodin also maintains that people in the state have an inherent right to private property, even in the state of the nature.

With regards to citizenship, Bodin hold the view that since family is the smallest unit of state, heads of families should be considered citizenship right including slaves, but maintained that they should, along with other citizens be under the sovereign rule of the state. Bodin also wanted that the nobles should be given a special position in social and political life of the state. It is, however, to be noted that everyone in the state, citizens, salves, traders. etc. who reside in the state are under the sovereign authority of the state.

With regards to law, he said that the law of nature is supreme and even the sovereign, the supreme ruler of state should not violate the law of nature. According to him, morality controlled law and regulates human conduct and behavior, but the law of nature controlled the conduct and affairs of the nation and, therefore, even the sovereign has to obey the law of nature as it is beyond human control. The underlying idea, therefore, is that only the law of nature is superior to the law of the sovereign or state.

Criticism

In the First place, Bodin's idea on the relation between state and family is not logical in the sense that he has failed to give a clear idea about the condition of the people in pre-political society. In the absence of a clear idea on the conditions of the people in the pre-political societies, it is difficult to accept his idea on the origin of the state which he traced to family.

In the second place, Bodin was not clear about the end and purpose of the state. Without having a clear idea on the purpose of the state it would be difficult to readily obey the command of the sovereign or state.

In the third place, though Bodin conceded that force also contribute to the formation of state, but how and why force contributed to the formation of state was not explained.

In the fourth place, Bodin has maintained that individual have inherent right to property, but at the same time he conferred absolute power to the state. How would the two right; right to private property and absolute power of the state be compromised, he did not give the explanation.

Lastly, he failed to define as to what natural needs gave rise to state over and above those supplied by the family and other groups.

Bodin's view on family as the origin of state:

Regarding family, Bodinmaintained that it is a natural institution, necessitated by the natural instinct of man and women. It is not only the first, but also inevitable form of human association. It is the oldest and the earliest social institution. Then, what is family? Bodin said that family is a group of individuals living under one roof headed by a senior most male member. Family, according to him, does not include slaves, but include property since property is inevitable for maintenance of family. Bodin, therefore, regarded property as a natural and necessary institution.

Bodin went further and said that family is a small unit of government in which man is the rightful natural ruler. Man is the ruler and the master of family because man is considered intellectually and morally superior to women. He, therefore, said man is the natural master and woman is a natural subject. This, he said, is the will of nature. It is the law of nature that the superior should rule over the inferior in the same way as reason rule over appetite.

There is no emancipation of woman from the rule of man. Bodin, however, said woman is not slave only she is subject to man.

Bodin maintained that family is the first natural form of state and the social instinct implanted in members brought them together. This same social instinct was also responsible for the formation of civil society. It was these civil societies which ultimately become state. But family is the first social institution which brought the state to come into existence. Bodin, therefor, traces the origin of state to family.

Conditions necessary for maintenance of state (Administration):

Bodin was aware of the possibility of revolution among the citizen which might threaten the stability of state. He said, therefore, that in order to avoid revolution, state must be well administered and well regulated. Wisdom or prudent will not guarantee stability. Stability of the state rather depends largely on the policy of the government.

In the first place, Bodin said, one should have a thorough understanding of the nature of the state. With the proper understanding of the nature of the state, it would be possible to know the drawback of the state or particular policy of the state for which it is unpopular. He said that inequality of possession, monopoly of offices by a particular class of people, exemption of taxation are resented to by the people and therefore, be avoided. He suggested that offices should never be made hereditary and as far as possible, there should be no disparity in the economic condition of the people. These are important measure to be adopted by the state to ensure stability of the state.

Bodin also maintained that, the existing law which people were accustomed to obey should not be changed suddenly. Enactment and legislation of law is easy but the implementation and enforcement is always a problem. People are already habituated to obey existing law, and that they find it difficult to adjust with new laws, how good they might be. A law may be good but useless if it is not obeyed.

Again Bodin suggested that state should maintain true religion as religion, he said, is the foundation of state. He, however, does not mention which religion is to be considered good. His idea was that fear of God instill in the minds of people the fear of wrong doing. His point is that a well organized state should have a well organized religion and should suppress any rebellious opponents. This is an important contributing factor for safe-guarding the stability of state.

Finally, Bodin suggested that state should not make any attempt to establish religion by force. That is, the prince must be tolerant in the affairs of religion. Any attempt to suppress any religion is only likely to result in rebellious conditions and will produce atheism in the state. However, Bodin is said to be advocating tolerant under particular circumstances or in a limited sense. Suppressive measure should be adopted, but the prince should know when to stop. The point here is tolerant would be based on expediency and not as a principle.

The above points are suggested by Bodin for the proper maintenance and administration of the state so as to avoid revolution for change of the system.

The ends of the state, according to Bodin

Regarding the ends of state,Bodin was in agreement with Aristotle. He accepted Aristotle's conception that state exists for life and continue to exist for the sake of good and honorable life. State aims at the realization of all good for the mind and body. In a well ordered and a well-organized sate, the government will concern itself first with justice, defence and then material welfare of the people. By this, Bodin means to say that provision of justice to the people and proper defence of the state should be the first consideration, and material welfare of the people must be secondary consideration. Bodin clearly stated that state and not rationality be conceived as existing for providing material welfare of the people. In a nutshell, however, Bodin said that provision of justice to the people, defense of the state for stability and safety, material welfare, and of course, the spiritual and intellectual development, constitute the ends of the state.

Bodin's Conception of Sovereignty

In the words of Bodin, sovereignty is supreme power over citizens and subjects unrestrained by law.From this definition of sovereignty it is clear that Bodin has given absolute power to the sovereign who is above all laws. It governs both individuals and society which exist in a state. The main object of this definition of sovereignty was unity of purpose and integration of state authority. Bodin tries to give a tangible and systemic explanation of what sovereignty actually is, and under what limitation and what restraint it should work. According to him, sovereignty originally lies with the people, but the need for common authority was felt by the people. The people then delegated their sovereign power to a single person who is called, the sovereign. Therefore, with regards to the origin of sovereignty, he said that sovereignty originated from the people.

Characteristics of Sovereignty

First, the sovereign is above law because he himself is the creator of law. Therefore, the sovereign cannot be within the purview of those laws which he himself created. The law of the land is simply the command of the sovereign. The primary attribute of the sovereign is the power to make law for citizens collectively and severally without the consent of none. The power of the sovereign is not limited to making of law, but extends to the control of customary law. Customary laws are allowed to exist only on the will of the sovereign.

Second, it is the sovereign, and the sovereign alone who has the power to declare war and conclude peace. The power for declaring war is not given to Generals in the bottle field, but they are carrying out the order of the sovereign only. He is the maker of war and maker of peace.

Third, the sovereign according to Bodin, is the sole authority to make appointment to public office. No state official have the authority to appoint principal public officers except with the consent of the sovereign. This implies that some high ranking officer may make appointment of officials with the approval of the sovereign. Even in this case, he is indirectly the appointing authority.

Fourth, since the sovereign is entrusted with absolute power over citizens and subjects, unrestrained by law, not a single individual has the right to resist his authority or question his order.

Fifth, the sovereign, being the maker of law, has the power to grant pardon and administer justice. In this sense, the sovereign is the sole legislators, the sole interpreter of law and the sole authority to enforce the law. In other words, the sovereign, according to Bodin is all in all in the state.

Sixth, sovereignty is perpetual and not meant for a any specific period. The sovereign as a person may die, but another sovereign will be created and the process will go on and on unless the state itself extinct.

Seventh, the sovereign may delegate some powers to other high ranking public officials but he cannot delegate the sovereign power to anyone. Therefore, Bodin said, sovereignty is inalienable and invincible.

Eighth, the sovereign is the head of the state and by virtue of this, he is the head of all other corporate associations within the state. He is the head of other associations because all other associations exist with the mercy of sovereign.

Limitation of the power of sovereign

Though Bodin talk about unlimited, inalienable and indivisible power of the sovereign, he himself contradicts his own and puts some limitation on the sovereign.

First, he said that the sovereign is bound by the principles of morality and law of nature. This implies, he himself admitted that the sovereign is bound by the law of God and the law of nature. He said that obedience to the law of nature is the moral duty of the sovereign. This is, however, not a legal obligation of the sovereign because there is no and there can be no legal means to compel the sovereign to obey the law of nature or divine law.

Therefore, obedience to divine law of nature depends on the conscience of the sovereign.

Second, the sovereign made promises to the people on his coronation day, which is kind of contract made with the people. Since the sovereign is subject to natural law he has to respect his contractual agreement with the people because contract is considered a natural law.

Third, Bodin himself admitted that there are certain social and constitutional restraints on the powers of the sovereign. The king or sovereign was the source of law, and at the same time, he was subject to certain constitutional laws which he cannot alter or change. Bodin was not clear about the difference between legal absolutism and political facts, and he did not make distinction between legality, morality and politics.

Fourth, Bodin believes in the inviolability of private property. Right to private property is guaranteed by the law of nature. Therefore, he said right to property is the natural right of individual and family. At the sometime, he advocated for the absolutism of thesovereign who he said was unrestrained by law. Here he was contradicting himself. At one time he said the sovereign was supreme and he was above law, he on the other occasion again said that the sovereign was subject to the law of nature, certain constitutional laws and some social customs and tradition.

Finally, Bodin also maintained the sovereign is bound by international law and international treaties in which he is a party. Therefore, the sovereign's international obligations put limitation to his power.

4

HOBBES, LOCKE, ROUSSEAU

A. Hobbes on human nature

Introduction:

A royalist, Thomas Hobbes was born in England in 1598. Being a royalist, he wrote a few pamphlets in support of royalty. When there was growing tension between the king and the parliament for contest of power, he fled to France. While he was in exiled, he published his famous work, 'Leveathan' in 1651. With the return of normalcy in England he returned to England in 1661.

Hobbe's writings were influenced by civil wars in Europe for overthrowing monarchy. He tried to exert influence on the people to support the absolute power of the monarch which, he felt is necessary to avoid civil war in England. His contention was that civil war would ruin and destroy England and the possible way to prevent England from such eventuality was veering all authorities to the monarch.

Thomas Hobbes, in support of the position of the royalty, developed his theory on human nature, law of nature and life in the state of nature (pre-political society). He maintains that man is inherently, naturally and essentially selfish. Man seeks self-gratification and self-glorification, and to that end, he does anything, including elimination of other competitors. Man seeks pleasure, and to ensure pleasure he wants to have the power, the power over the others. However, Hobbes maintains that man are born equal or roughly equal in mental and physical strength. Therefore, it was not possible to dominate and over powered others. In the process, man entered into conflict with one another leading to a virtual society of war and conflict. He, however, admitted that men do not always have physical confrontation, yet there constantly exists a spirit of competition among them because of which there is a constant fear of war. Competition among men for power and glory, who are roughly equal in power and strength leads to war, and therefore, society in the state of nature was characterized by Hobbes as 'solitary, poor, nasty, brutish, and short'. In such a state, every man is against every man, everyman is the enemy of every man.

Regarding the law of nature or natural law, he said the only law which was known to natural man was the law of the jungle, the law of the survival of the fittest. This was the only law that ruled the state of nature. There was no authority to frame rules and regulation nor was there authority to enforce. The only order of the day was, "Kill, whom you can, and take what you can".

Thomas Hobbes has given the characteristics of natural state as follows:

i. There is no distinction between right or wrong. In other words, the concept of right or wrong does not simply exist in such natural state nor there was any standard of measurement to decide what is right and what is wrong.

ii. There is no distinction between the just and the unjust. In other words, where there is no authority/common authority to decide the just and unjust, the question of justice simply does not exist. What a man think is just according to his selfish perception, it is just to him. But what a man call just may not be just to another.

iii. In the state of nature, there cannot exist the institution of private property, because in such society, might is right and that there is always a risk for one to loss his property at the hands of the physically superiors. Therefore, there is absolutely no security of life and property in the state of nature.

Therefore, it is evident from the above discussion that, Thomas Hobbes attributed the horrific nature of life in the state of nature to the selfish nature of man.

NATURAL RIGHTS AND NATURAL LAWS:

Thomas Hobbes makes a distinction between natural right and natural law. By natural right, he said it means the right and liberty that every individual do what he thinks would best do for his own preservation. On the other hand, natural law implies, he said, certain restraints and restrictions by reason. It is by the law of nature that man is obliged to renounce some part of his claim for the realization of a better and a more meaningful life. State of nature is a state of war because everyman in there have the same equal right. To make life more secured and more meaningful, the natural law is being devised according to which man is to seek peace and observe certain moral restraints. But again, Hobbes said, this is possible only when man abandons his natural rights to all things. This abandonment of natural rights must, however, be mutual and reciprocal. Each man must agree with the others to refrain from exercising his natural liberty and keeps the promises he made. Justice is the keeping of promises made and injustice is the failure to keep promises. But Thomas Hobbes said, promises are always made by selfish man to satisfy his selfish motive. Therefore, there is no guarantee that man would keep his promises.In other words, a selfish and self-centered who makes all promises with selfish motives will certainly, one day or the other, breaks his promises the moment he found that things move against his interest. Therefore, there must be a competent authority to compel him to keep his promises.

SOCIAL CONTRACT:

Thomas Hobbes after having developed his theory of human nature, natural law, state of nature and natural rights proceeds to develop his theory of social contract which is fundamentally different from that of earlier contracts developed by earlier writers. In the case of earlier contracts, the contracts were made between the people and the sovereign. But, Hobbes' contract was purely a contract entered into by the people, among the people and for the people. It is a contract by which people created and the state is the result of the contract.

Hobbes' social contract is two tier contracts. First, by institution, i.e. men, out of their impulse unite to create a civil society. Second, by acquisition i.e. a superior power threatens men with destruction and the fear of men for being destroyed and eliminate compel them to unite and seek peace. Out of the two, the first is cent percent social contract and the second is fifty percent contract. The point here is, it is not the desire for power and glory that compels men to enter into a contract, but rather it is the desire for securing security of life and property that induces men to make a contract among themselve.

Hobbes is a rationalist and believes that reason is an integral part of man. Man, by reason, realizes the futility of living in a constant and perpetual fear of death and destruction. Then man by reason, could accept the principle of not doing to others which they think is unreasonable to be done to thyself. Therefore, man enters into a contract with others not to do to one another what he would not wish to have been done to himself. Thus, social impulse is not the first cause for the creation of state or civil society. On the other hand, it is man's desire for self-preservation which is responsible for the formation of state.

Thomas Hobbes writes "A commonwealth is said to be constituted when a multitude of men agreed and covenanted everyone with everyone, that this man or the assembly of men would be the sovereign". In the contract everyman would say, "I authorize and give up my right of governing myself to this man or to this assembly of men on this condition that thou give up thy right to him and authorize all his actions in like manner". Thus, men enter into a contract, not to do to one another what they would not wish to have been done to themselves. But Man's desire for power, glory, self-preservation continues to haunt the contract making at a constant risk of breaking up. Therefore, there is a need for some restraining power, strong enough to compel man to keep the terms of contract; there should be one sovereign authority vested with all powers.

With regards to the questions, who are the parties to the contract, he said the parties to the contract are individual natural men and not the people as a group. The sovereign is not a party to the contract, but he is the creation of the contract. In other words, individual is the creator of the sovereign. The state that was created out of social contract is a single personality taking the place of many individuals. This single personality is the sovereign who determines the commonwealth. This, Hobbes said, is the origin of state and from whom people got peace and security.

Hobbes' social contract theory is an explanatory myth which he used to justify the absolute power of the state. It is an explanatory myth to explain why men should submit to the authority of the state. It is a pure fiction though had much influence on much people for many centuries.

CRITICISM:

i. Hobbes makes fear to be the strongest basis of contract. Fear is that which contributes to the making of the contract. But which particular fear makes it man to make a contract, whether it is the fear of losing life or losing one's property. He was not vividly clear about it. He was certainly exaggerating fear factor and misunderstood its nature. Fear is uncertain and that it cannot be the only basis of modern state.

ii. Hobbes certainly laid too much emphasis on distrust. He said, it was mutual distrust among men which induces men to enter into a contract. But, equally important is the existence of usual cooperation among men. How a man whom he characterizes as brutish, nasty etc. would suddenly come to reason and agreed to lead a life of peace and cooperation. In fact, a contract is the product of society and the society is not the product of a contract.

B. JOHN LOCKE

John Locke was born in England in 1632 and died in 1704. As he had suffered persecution under the Stuarts, he wanted a change in the government through revolution. He, then become the apostle of the famous bloodless revolution called the Glorious Revolution of 1658. His most important work, "Two Treatises on Civil Government" was devoted for justification of revolution for change of authoritarian government.

Human Nature and State of Nature:

Unlike Hobbes, Locke maintains that a natural man is not without reason. Even in the state of nature man is guided by morality and reason. Locke takes a positive view of man and his nature. He said, each man lived a peaceful life and are free and equal. To him, each lived according to his own liking, independent of other. There was peace, goodwill, mutual cooperation and mutual preservation. He lived a peaceful life under the guidance and supervision of reason with morality and the earth and everything that lived in it and the animal that feed upon it, all belong to men in common. The state of nature, he said, is not a state of war, but rather it was a state of liberty. Anything that nature had offered to mankind are equally shared and enjoyed by the people in common. No man, he said, could claim exclusive ownership over anything that nature has offered. In such state of nature there was no special privileges to any group of people, there was no government nor law regulating human conduct.

The state of nature as depicted by Locke was not a state of savages but a community of virtuous anarchists who do not required police and law courts, because they are guided by reason. To Locke, reason is another name for law, natural law and state of nature is a perfect state wherein there is freedom and equality. Since Locke's state of nature is a state wherein people lived a peaceful and meaningful life. What would then be the different between state of nature and civil society? The answer Locke has given is that, in the state of nature there are the imperfections – partial judgment inadequate force to execute and enforce the decision of judiciary and a legislature to make uniform rules. Therefore, Locke said, as a remedy to these imperfections, men surrendered their natural rights to a common authority. He looks at such state as a stage through which men had to essentially go through.

LAW OF NATURE

Locke maintains that there is the law of nature which governs human conduct. Reason, which everyone has, controls the action of everyone. Therefore, reason or law of nature, according him, is the foundation on which he developed his political philosophy. In the second edition of his work, 'Treatise on Civil Government' he mentioned his theory on the law of nature.

In the first place, he said, the law of nature is the Law of Equality which provides no privileges to anyone. It is the law of perfect equality and freedom. Man is absolutely free to do what he wants to do so long as such action do not hurt others in their enjoyment of their natural rights. It is man's natural reason which guides man to do or not to do a thing. Therefore, reason in man makes man to be rational in his action. The fundamental principle of natural law's not only the preservation of society, but also the preservation of everyone in the society.

In the second place the law of nature enjoins the practice of truth and keeping of faith. It is by the law of nature that Adam and Eve, after them, all parents were under the obligation to look after their children, and in return children were, by the law of nature and the law of God, to honour, protect and look after their parents as they grow old.

In the third place, he said, by the law of nature, no man has the authority, right and power over the life, liberty and possessions of others.

In the fourth place, he said, by the law of nature, people have the right to revolution.

Finally, Locke maintains that people have the natural right to property and by the same natural right they must respect the property of one another.

SOCIAL CONTRACT

Locke maintains that, people in the state of nature lived a peaceful and happy life having freedom and equality. But the question is what then prompted men to give up their natural rights and liberty. Locke has given the answer – The state of nature was deficient in three important respects.

1. The state of nature was full of doubts and difficulties. All men do not follow the command of reason, and men are sometimes blinded by momentary advantages and do not always recognized general interests. They are guided by prejudices and partisan feelings. Therefore, it was necessary to establish a common authority to make law to determine what is just and what is unjust. It was this necessity which brings into existence the civil society or state.

2. There is no third and natural party to decide dispute among men. Therefore, state was created to be a deciding authority in such cases.
3. In the state of nature there was no authority to punish any offender. Therefore, men entered into a contract and created an authority in which they surrendered their rights of judgment. This common authority so created out of a contract would decide cases according to law agreed upon.

It is, therefore evident that civil government, according Locke is the result of a contract. The civil authority is neither the gift of God nor the gift of nature but purely created on contractual will of men. He maintains that each individual entered into a contract with one another to create a community. This contract, he said, was made for the protection and preservation of property. Locke said, each individual surrendered some of their natural rights while retaining the rest, not to individual or group of individuals, but to the common as a whole and in which is vested a political authority. The party to the contract, he said were the people on the one hand and the community or authority on the other.

The social contract theory of John Locke as seen above is a two way contract. The civil society was the product of the contract and also a party to the contract and was bound by the terms of the contract in the same way as the individuals are. As per the terms of the contract, individuals would receive protection of their life and property in return for giving up some of their natural rights to the civil authority. The civil authority has the obligation to protect the life and property of individuals. Therefore, it is clear that Locke, by developing his political philosophy wanted to establish a civil government accountable to the people i.e. liberal democratic form of government.

C. JEAN JACQUES ROUSSEAU

Rousseau was born in the city of Geneva on June 28, 1712. During his lifetime, he accomplished many things including mastery in writing on music, politics and education. His fame primarily rested on his writings. His father was a watch maker. The death of his mother while he was born disintegrated his family. His parents were protestant but he converted into Catholicism under the influence of Madame Wares. He died in 1778.

State of Nature

Rousseau maintains that the state of nature was not a state of war and conflict. Man in the state of nature, he said, enjoys a perfect and absolute freedom and liberty. It was a state of completely anarchic individual freedom and its essential characteristic is that, man lives an isolated life, isolated from his fellow men.

He maintains that though man was non-social in the state of nature, he possessed an undeveloped capacity of morality and reason. In such primitive natural state, there was no inequality, suppression and oppression of man by man, there was no poverty as nature has given the needs of man in plenty. Therefore, Rousseau has depicted life in the state of nature as peaceful, prosperous and pleasant with no-bound.

However, a question arises, why a natural man in a natural state having and enjoying a perfect peaceful and happy life should leave the state of nature, and create a civil state by contract. The answer Rousseau has given to this question is, men were driven to form a society as a result of nature's fury like floods, volcanic eruptions, earthquakes. These nature's fury befalling on men necessitated unified and collective action making social life inevitable. In the natural state, man was guided by two sentiments – self-interest and pity. Having no legal or moral obligation with others, man could not be good or bad or virtuous or vicious. Therefore, he maintains that a natural man in the natural state was an animal, and his actions and behavior are guided by instinct. Selfishness, regard for opinion of others, arts, slavery, paternal affection exists in man only after he comes in contact with other fellow men. In other words, love, hatred, selfishness etc. come into surface only when men started living together in group as social being.

SOCIAL CONTRACT THEORY

Roussean's theory of social contract is basically based on Locke's Treatise on Government with the exception of some variations here and there. For both Locke and Rousseau, social contract is the basis of political society and the ground of political obligation. Both of them defend revolutions. In fact Locke's philosophy is the main source of inspiration for Rousseau to develop his own social contract.

However, there is a fundamental difference between Locke's and Rousseau's social contract, particularly with regards to the parties to the contract. According to Rousseau, the contract is between the individuals in their corporate capacity. Individuals, say, a,b,c etc. surrender all their natural rights to the collective whole – a+b+c+d etc. In this contract, he said no one is a loser, but everybody is a gainer, for when anyone is attacked the whole society comes to his rescue.

The contract, according to Rousseau is not between the king and the people, but among the people themselves. The sovereign so created out of the contract is not the king or a single individual or group of individuals, but rather, the peoples are the real sovereign. He was actually speaking about popular sovereignty. The king is only the agent of the sovereign, i.e. the people. The individuals surrendered, not some, but all their natural rights to the whole community and not to any particular individual. Therefore, the people or the community as a whole is the real sovereign and the king is only the titular sovereign. The king is merely the agent of the sovereign and could be removed at any time without assigning any reason thereof.

Rousseau also maintains like Hobbes, that man gave up all their natural right and prerogatives to the state. The social contract, he said, ordains the total surrender to the whole community without condition. The individual can no longer claim anything as nature gives everyman an absolute power over his limb, so also the contract gives the body politics absolute power over all its members.

The underlying idea of Rousseau, however, is that each individual surrenders himself, not to any particular man or group of men but to the community as a whole in which he himself is a member. In other words, individuals constitute the sovereign by becoming member of state. He said, each gives himself up to himself and state is the master of himself. "I surrender all myself. I receive only a fraction of the sovereignty of the community, and ultimately I am the thousand part of a tyrant and i am also the whole of a slave. Leviathan is still Leave than, even though it is a corporate."

General will

The concept of general wills occupies a central position in the political philosophy of Rousseau. Patrick Riley said, Rousseau himself insists that 'general will is always right,' that it is 'the will that one has as a citizen' when one think of the common good and not of one's own particular will as a private person". Subsequent writers have also used the distinction between particular will and general will. The existence of these had two types of will i.e. actual will and real will. Actual will is always, according to Rousseau, motivated by a person's immediate and selfish interest. Real will, on the other hand, he said, is motivated by the ultimate collective interest. Actual will is reflected in his 'lower self and real will is reflected in his highest self'. Actual will is directed towards gratification of man's desires while real will will directs man to act reasonably. Actual will is unstable, mutable and inconsistent, and it changes from time to time and from place to place. On the other hand, Rousseau opines that real will is stable, constant, consistent and determinate, determinate to the common good. Man's freedom, he said consists in overcoming his actual will and in following man's direction to real will. Real will is the expression of true freedom and subordinates man's selfish interest and motive to the interest of the community which is shared by all in the community. Therefore, it appears that, a sum total of real will of individual is the General will.

However, Rousseau admitted that man has inherent weakness and imperfection to suppress his actual will. This problem, he said, could be solved by transition from particular will. The general will is capable of harmonizing the interest of each with those of all. It does not represent a compromise or convergence of diverse interest but an expression of the highest will in everyman. It is a spirit of citizenship in its concrete shape. While man's particular will may create or tend to create confusion, general will in him guide him in the right way. It is, therefore, necessary and expedient for man to follow the right way so as to secure and enjoy his true freedom. In other words, when man acts in the state against his particular will under the direction of his general will, he is not losing his freedom. In fact, the constraint of general will is instrumental for securing his ultimate freedom, which reconciles freedom of each with freedom of all. It is in this context that Rousseau said, 'man can be forced to be free' which means, man can be forced to follow the general will.

The ultimate political implication of Rousseau's general will is the establishment of popular sovereignly or if you like direct democracy of real will of all the members of the community. In other words, in the civil society where men are made (or forced) to follow their higher self only, their character is fundamentally transformed.

Rousseau's influence on modern thought-philosophy as well as literature-is unmatched. His slogan "Return to Nature" inspired nineteenth-century romantic poetry in English which further influenced Indian poetries in early decades of the twentieth century. His philosophical ideas were the main source of inspiration behind the French Revolution (1789) which declared "liberty, equality, fraternity" as its goal. Rousseau's theory of the General will was adopted by eminent English political philosophers like T.H. Green (1836-82), L.T. Hobhouse (1864-1929) and Ernest Barker (1874-1960) to develop their respective moral and political philosophies. Rousseau's concept of the 'popular sovereignty' is regarded as the keynote of the contemporary democratic theory.

LucioColletti (From Rousseau to Lenin: Studies in Ideology and Society; 1972) interpreted Rousseau's philosophy in terms of understanding the origin and nature of Modern Capitalism. According to this view, Rousseau identified three phases of economic development of society: (a) Early phase which marks the emergence of the simple subsistence economy of the primitive man;(b) Intermediate phase which is characterized by the 'Patriarchal state' evolved from the necessity of meeting human needs collectively, and promoted by the technological progress; and finally, (c) Capitalist phase which involves the division of labour, private property, exchange relationships, etc. It transpires from Rousseau's writings that originally the fruits of earth belonged to all, and the earth belonging to none. The man who enclosed a piece of ground and declared it to be 'his' own, created 'private property' and civil society. Capitalism denotes the pursuit of private interest; private ownership, possession and appropriation of property. Exchange relationship promoted by the capitalism involves using other individuals as 'tools' for serving one's self-interest, that is exploitation of others, It is basically unjust and demoralizing, resulting in competition and conflict.

Adam Smith (1723-90), Rousseau's contemporary British philosopher, believed that the pursuit of individual well-being by each member of the society would result in general well-being. On the contrary, Rousseau argued that material progress of civilization (based on competition, conflict and exploitation) led to dehumanization. In fact Rousseau was primarily concerned with the decadence of 'moral values' rather than exposing the exploitative character of commodity production. Hence, he could not suggest the way to transcendence of capitalism by a superior form of economy without its evils. He could only suggest a system of small peasant proprietors which was quite unfit for adoption in the modern age. Relevance of Rousseau should, therefore, be sought in the realm of moral and political thought rather than economic thought. He particularly drew attention to the following defects of the civil society. It legitimized inequality and made it irrevocable; it led to wrong socialization of man, obstructing his free self-development (this was the problem of education); and it caused alienation of man. That is why Rousseau is, sometimes, regarded as a forerunner of Young Marx, as represented in Marx's Economic and Philosophic Manuscripts of 1844. It is interesting to note that the contemporary critical theory (a stream of Neo-Marxism) which seeks to secure human emancipation by containing man's dependence on technology recognizes Rousseau as its source of inspiration. "Slaves become so debased by their chains as to lose even the desire of breaking from them".Jean-Jacques Rousseau (The Social Contract, 1762)

ALIENATION

A State of mind in which individual is isolated from the significant aspects of his social existence or from the creative aspects of his own personality. Young Marx identified alienation as a characteristic of the capitalist system, particularly because under this system labour was treated as a factor of production rather than an expression of human personality.

Democrat or Totalitarian

Rousseau postulates absolute sovereignty of the 'General Will'. Liberal thinkers treat 'will' as the basis of the state.

'Will' in this sense is supposed to be morally neutral. But Rousseau's concept of the General Will is not so. General Will represents the point of convergence of the real will of all members of the community. Real will itself is morally superior to actual will; these two represent individual's higher self and lower self respectively. Rousseau holds that individual gets his true freedom by obeying the dictates of his real will; this authority is now transferred to the General Will. When individual obeys the command of the General Will, he may be required to suppress his actual will (i.e. temptation toward momentary pleasure or profit). For this paradoxical situation, Rousseau prescribes a paradoxical solution: "Man can be forced to be free".

Some writers tend to interpret this statement to imply that Rousseau gives unbridled power to the state which enables it to exercise total control over all aspects of his life. So they allege that Rousseau was a totalitarian, J.L. Talmon (The Rise of Totalitarian Democracy;1961) dubbed Rousseau the intellectual forerunner of twentieth-century totalitarianism. Leon Duguit (1859-1928) described Rousseau as the source of inspiration for the absolutist doctrine of Immanuel Kant (1724-1804) and G.W.F. Hegel (1770-1831), German philosophers. Bertrand Russell (1872-1970) observed that Hitler's ideology was the culmination of Rousseau's thinking. Alfred Cobban (1901-68) pointed out that the idea of dictatorship is the logical and historical outcome of the democratic theory of the General Will. On the other hand, some commentators have drawn attention to Rousseau's profound faith in human freedom. G.D.H Cole (1889-1959) argued that Rousseau regards will, not force the legitimate basis of social obligation. A.D. Lindsay (1879-1952) thinks that Rousseau's idea of the General Will accords priority to the sense of sociability.

These writers believe that respect for freedom is the keynote of Rousseau's moral and political philosophy.

However, on closer analysis, it is revealed that Rousseau is basically a democrat sincerely devoted to human emancipation, and not a totalitarian inclined toward suppression of human freedom. As a thinker, he felt drawn to the lowly, the weak, and the oppressed and proclaimed liberty, justice and equality as the ends of law and government. His theory of absolute sovereignty of the General Will simply implies that man should submit to law and government when it is thoroughly committed to ultimate good of the whole community. Moreover, totalitarianism is a late modern concept which seeks to dominate all spheres of men's life-political, economic, social, cultural, educational, artistic, and so on; it tends to use all possible means of regimentation- propaganda, concentration camps, brainwashing and side spread terror, etc. How can we club Rousseau with such activities, for he was a man who always pleaded for generosity and clemency and humanity?

5

KARL MARX, LENIN AND HEGEL

A. KARL MARX DIALECTICAL MATERIALISM

Dialectical materialism represents the philosophical foundation of Marxism. Karl Marx, while rejecting Hegel's belief that idea or consciousness was the essence of the universe said 'matter' was the essence of the universe, which embodied the force behind all manifestations of the social change. According to Karl Marx, every stage of social development and progress represented the corresponding material progress of a society. In other words, Karl Marx maintains that materialism and not idealism as Hagel advocated, is that represents human progress. This is called dialectical materialism of Karl Marx. Matter and not Idea is that which condition human development.

As a matter of fact, Hagel could claim the ownership of dialectical method, and even Karl Marx adopted this method to study his materialism. He combines Hegel's dialectic method with his own philosophy of materialism. The term, 'dialectic or dialectical' originally referred to the process whereby ideas are formed and clarified in the course of intellectual debate. A proposition or thesis is first advanced or put forward which is then challenged and countered with the counter-proposition, or antithesis. Since both the proposition are equally partly right, a compromise proposition could be reached which becomes the synthesis. The synthesis combines in it the valid and true elements of the two thesis i.e. the thesis and the antithesis.

Hegel puts up the proposition that social institutions only reflect the idea behind them, and that, it is the movement of ideas, through a dialectical process, which is responsible for the development of social institutions. He believes that nation states are the result of the social evolution, which is an embodiment of truth, "the march of God on earth". It is a perfect form of social institutions. Karl Marx, while agreeing with Hegel on the mechanism of social change, the framework of thesis, antithesis and synthesis, refused to agree with him on the idea that of consciousness as the real force behind social evolution. He, however, believes that social institutions are shaped and guided by material conditions of human life which, he further said, are conditioned by the mode of production and distribution in a society. The truth is that Karl Marx replaced Hegel's dialectical idealism with dialectical materialism.

Karl Marx has consistently believes that dialectic was a powerful logical method capable of demonstrating a law of social change and development, and in consequence his philosophy, like Hegel's was a philosophy of history. Though Marx construed his philosophy as a form of materialism, he used the dialectic to support a theory of social change and progress in which higher moral values are necessarily realized. Karl Marx also believes that the driving force of social change is struggle, and the determining factor in the last resort is power. The struggle, he said, is a struggle between social classes rather than nations, and the power is economic rather than political because power he said, is the consequence of economic domination of one social class over the other. The application of the laws of dialectic in social life is demonstrated in his theory of historical materialism.

Historical materialism or materialistic interpretation of history

While dialectical materialism is the philosophical foundation of Karl Marx's philosophy, historical materialism is the empirical basis of his historical materialism. In other words, dialectical materialism is the subject of philosophical speculation, but historical materialism is a subject of social and historical investigation like an empirical science.

At the very outset, historical materialism implies that at any given period, the economic relation of society, that is, the means whereby men and women provide for their sustenance, produce; exchange and distribute, the thesis that they regard necessary for the satisfaction of their needs – exert a preponderant influence in shaping the progress of the society, that is, moulding of social, political, intellectual and ethical relationship. In other words, Karl Marx attributes all kinds of social relation and progress at any stage of historical development to the economic conditions.

Karl Marx maintains that the survival of man depends entirely on how he was able to produce his material needs. It is, therefore, he said, production and production process is the most important human activity and society itself comes into existence for the maximization of production. This is because he said man in association with others, could produce more others as compared to man in isolation. A perfect society is a society that which secure all the necessities of life to the satisfaction of all its members. However, Karl Marx maintains that perfection has to come through a very long dialectical process of conflict between antagonistic elements in the society. History, according to him, is nothing, but the history of conflicts and antagonism between different classes in the society resulting from the defective system of mode of production and distribution. Therefore, according to Marx, it is the economic conditions of the people which dominated and determined the social political and religious life of people, and society as a whole.

Since, he said, material production is the key to man's life changes in this process are responsible for all historical development. This is what he called historical materialism. Karl Marx said, "In the social production of their life, men enter into a definite relation that are indispensible and independent of their will and relation of production which correspond to a definite stage of development of their productive forces. The sum total of their relations of production constitutes the economic structure, the real base on which rises a legal and political super structure " According to this interpretation, the mode of production in a given society constitutes its base or sub-structure, legal and morals constitute its super-structure which are shaped according to the changing character of the base or sub-structure.

At certain stage of development, Karl Marx said, the material productive forces of society come in conflict with the existing relation of production. This conflict then turned into a social revolution which ultimately culminated into a violent class conflict. In order to understand this process, it would be necessary to differentiate between the forces of production and relation of production. By forces of production Marx means to say, means of production like tools, machineries, factories etc. and labour power i.e. man power like skill, experience, expertise, knowledge which are involved in the process of production. Relations of production are constituted by the pattern of economic ownership of the means of production. Therefore, at every stage of historical development owners of means of production constitute the dominant class and those who are directly engaged as laborer constitute the dependent class though they are numerically larger.

Karl Marx also maintains that the process of historical development can also be explained by dialectical method. According to this method, the existing or established order is the thesis which inevitably produced its own antithesis because of its inherent internal contradictions in the form of a new mode of production. That is to say that, with the introduction of new technique of production resulting from fast industrialization, production increases resulting in the emergence of internal contradiction. This internal contradiction produces a new revolutionary class for the overthrows of the existing system, and the old order gives way to the new, that is, slave society is replaced by feudal society and the feudal society is replaced by the capitalist society. Karl Marx looks at the capitalist society as imperfect and full of contradictions which would bring about its own destruction. There exists in the system the two antagonistic classes- the haves and the have nots, the bourgeoisies and the proletariat, the dominant and the dependent classes and the consequent exploitation of the have nots by the haves. Therefore, this inherent contradiction in the capitalist system is bound to produce a violent revolution resulting to the destruction of the system and the establishment of a new system- the rule of the working class and consequently, the establishment of a stateless society.

Karl Marx's doctrine of historical materialism, in a nutshell, therefore, means that history is not the history of great men, it is not the history of war and the making of peace, but rather, it is the history of who owned and who do not owned. It is the history of conflict between different social classes due to the control of means of production and distribution. It is the history of how an economically dominant class is also politically dominant class. History, therefore, is about the history of how a much numerical larger working class are economically, politically and socially exploited by the much smaller capitalist class, which Karl Marx said, would inevitably lead to violent revolution for over throwing the capitalist regime.

B. LENIN'S THEORY OF IMPERIALISM

Lenin (Vladimir Illch Lenin (1870-1924) was an eminent Marxist revolutionary who led the Bolshevic party in Russian Revolution (1917) Lenin's name is associated with a particular interpretation of Marxism which was described as Marxism – Lenism and which was adopted as the official ideology of the former Soviet Union (USSR)

Theory of Imperialism:

Different writers and philosophers, have given different meanings and interpretation to the term Imperialism. Ebensein, speaking about imperialism said, "Love of oneself becomes hatred, of thesis and enslavement of others is clothed in such a mark as the white man's burden and the need for living space'. Even highly democratic nations at one time or other have fallen victims to the diseases of imperialism. "To some scholars, imperialism is a form of exploitation through political domination of weaker nations by powerful nations. To other, it is a sacred duty which must not be shirked by the advance countries of the world in relation to backward countries. Both these views are extreme. A well-planned and carefully worked out plan of ruthless exploitation of backward regions is as foreign to general history of imperialism as conscious civilizing mission typified in the much abused phrase, "The white man's burdens".

Lenin maintains that capitalism is the sole cause of imperialism. In his words, "If it were necessary to give the briefest possible definition of imperialism, we should have to say that imperialism is the monopoly stage of capitalism". By imperialism, he refers to the policy, practice or process through which an advanced nation uses its military, political or economic power to expand its rule and extend its control over backward, distant political communities for the sole purpose of extracting economic gain, military security and international prestige as well as establishing its cultural domination over other nations. In his work, 'Imperialism-The higher state of capitalism, 1916, he maintains that imperialism was an economic necessarily of capitalist economy. In his view, when capital accumulation in a capitalist country rises to such an extent that it cannot all find its profitable use within its own territory, then it is forced to look abroad for profitable outlets.

Lenin has given three driving forces behind imperialist expansion: search for new spheres for investment, new market for finished goods and new source for raw materials for new industries, foreign trade, according to him, allows the capitalists to secure high rate of return than domestic trade. Overseas investment opens up new sources of labour and markets, and allows access to raw materials at a very cheap price. Marx and Engels maintain that since capitalism represented higher stage of social development than feudalism, they were not averse to this trend. Lenin reinterpreted this trend as a trend of exploitation of the poor nations by the rich nations, and therefore, he condemned imperialism. He divides nations into the oppressed and oppressors which is the essence of his imperialism. Imperialism has similarity with capitalist system of society in which society was divided into exploiting and exploited classes. He exhorted all oppressed and exploited nations all over the world to unite against the oppressor nations and play the role of revolutionary proletariat against the oppressive capitalist nations.

He looks at the world war, the First World War as the design of powerful capitalist states to perpetuate and further their policy of colonization of the underdeveloped Asian and African countries so that they can extract more raw materials needed for their industries at home. War was the instrument used by them to further their economic interest. Therefore, Lenin maintains that powerful nations of Europe fought among themselves in the process of their competition for controlling the weak and underdeveloped Asian and African countries so that they gain maximum economic benefits.Imperialism, therefore, is a new form of colonialism adopted by powerful European countries to perpetuate and further their exploitation. This is what Lenin calls, 'Imperialism'.

C. HEGEL (George Wilhelm Friedrich Hegel)

Hegel, (1770-1831) a German Philosopher who was one of the chief exponents' of idealism. He was born in a middle class protestant family. Right from his childhood, he was deeply interested in philosophy. He took teaching as his profession and served at several universities in Switzerland and Germany. He served in the University of Berlin till he died in 1831.

Hegel authored many books to his credit of which the following are worth mentioning:

1. Phenomenology of Spirit (1507).
2. The Science of Logic (1812).
3. Encyclopedia of Philosophical Sciences (1817).
4. Philosophy of Right (1821). Hegelian Dialectic

The Term 'dialectic' is derived from Greek word which refers to 'the method of investigation of truth through the art of disputation', that is, by the process of argument and counter-argument. This means, truth, ultimate truth, and could be realized through and by the process of argument and counter argument. Hegel applied this method to identify the process whereby contradictions are resolved for arising at a higher truth. Hegel described this process in terms of 'thesis' (the initial idea), the 'anti-thesis' the opposite idea and the 'synthesis' (the idea or ideal that comes out from the clash between the thesis and the antithesis). However, Hegel maintains that the initial synthesis is not perfect and that there would be opposition and contradictions which will go on repeating itself until it reaches the stage of ultimate truth.

Therefore, the central idea of Hegelian dialectic is that the initial idea or proposition or what he calls thesis does not in any way represent the ultimate truth, and there is a counter –idea or proposition or antithesis which is a negation of the thesis. However, this counter-proposition or negation neither represents the ultimate truth nor it is a perfect proposition. Therefore, there is argument and counter argument which, goes on, until the untrue elements in both are destroyed a disappeared. With the disappearance of all the untrue elements in both, there comes into existence the final and ultimate truth which Hegel calls the 'Synthesis', However, the new synthesis is yet far from reaching perfect truth, arguments and counter arguments go on, and the process of negation of negation continues till it reaches the stage - perfect truth, free from all contradictions.

Hegel's dialectical method occupies a central position in his political philosophy. His main focus was how to solve contradictions and oppositions in the society. As an idealist, he believes that idea is that which is important and by adopting dialectical method the ultimate idea of perfect truth could be arrived at.

REFERENCES

Ackrill, J.L. :Aristotle the Philosopher, Oxford, Oxford University Press, 1975.

AGARWAL R.C.: Political theory (Principles of Political Science), 2008.

Allan, D.J. : The Philosophy of Aristotle, Oxford, Oxford University Press, 1970.

Andrews, A. : The Greek Society, Harmondsworth, Penguins, 1967.

Ashcraft,R. : Revolutionary Politics and Locke's Two Treatises of Government, Political Theory, Vol. 8,99. 429-485, 1980.

ASIRVATHAM EDDY revised by K.K. Misra: Political Theory,1998.

Barker, E. : Social Contract, Oxford, Oxford University Press, 1948.

Barker : The Politics of Aristotle, Translated with introduction, Notes and Appendix, London, Oxford University Press, 1979.

Barker : Aristotle's Politics, Oxford, Oxford University Press, 1995.

Bobonich, C. : Plato's Utopia Recast: His Later Ethics and Politics, Oxford, Oxford University Press, 2002.

Carver, T. : Marx and Engels: The Intellectual Relationship, Brighton, Harvester, 1983.

Carver, T.: The Question of Jean-Jacques Rousseau, New Haven, Yale University Press, 1989.

Catlin, G. : Thomas Hobbes as Philosopher, Publicist and Man of Letters, Oxford, Clarendon Press, 1922.

Chapman, J.W. : Rousseau – Totalitarian or Liberal? New York, Columbia University Press, 1956.

Conford, EM. : Plato's Theory of Knowledge, New York, Humanities Press, 1945.

Cohen, G.A. : Karl Marx's Theory of History: A Defence, Oxford, Oxford University Press, 1979.

Cole, G.D.H : A History of Socialist Thought, 5 Vols., London, Macmillan, 1956.

Coleman, F.M. : Hobbes and America: Exploring the Constitutional Foundations, Toronto, University of Toronto Press, 1977.

Coleman, J. : A History of Political Thought, Oxford, Blackwell Publishers, 2000.

Craston, M. (Ed.): Western Political Philosophers, London, Fontana, 1964.

Crossman, R. : Plato Today, London, Allen &Unwin, 1939.

Curtis, M. : The Great Political Theories, 2 Vols. New York, Avon, 1961.

DAS P.G. Modern Political Theory, 2009.

Dahl, R.A. : Political Theory today, World Politics, XI, October, pp. 89-102, 1958.

Dunn, J. : The Political Thought of John Locke-An Historical Account of the Argument of the Two Treatise of Government, Cambridge, Cambridge University Press,1968a.

Dunn, J: Justice and the Interpretation of Locke's Political Theory, Political Studies, Vol 16, pp 68-87, 1968b.

Durkheim, E. : Montesquieu and Rousseau, Ann Arbor, University of Michigan Press, 1960.

Fine, G (Ed.) : Plato, 2 Vol., Oxford, Oxford University Press, 1999.

Friedrich, C.J. : The Philosophy of Hegel, New York, Modern Library, 1953.

122-134, 1978.

GAUBA OP: Western Political Thought, 2011.

GAUBA O.P.: An Introduction to Political Theory (5TH Edition), 2009.

Gilbert, A.H.: Machiavelli's Prince and its Forerunners, Durham, NC, Duke University Press, 1938.

Gunnell, J.G.: The myth of the tradition, American Political Science Review, Vol. 72, pp.

Hampsher-Monk, I.W : The Political Philosophy of Edmund Burke, London, Longman, 1987.

Hook, S.: Towards an Understanding of Karl Marx, New York, John Day, 1933.

Jowett, B.: Aristotle's The Politics, Oxford, Clarendon Press, 1905.

Klosko, G.: The Development of Plato's Political Theory, New York, Methuen, 1986.

Lawson, G.: Examination of the Political Part of Mr. Hobbs, His Leviathan, London, The Silver Library, 1657.

Lasswell, H.: Politics Who Gets What, When, and How, New York, McGraw- Hill, 1936.

Marshall, J.: John Locke: An Historical Account of the Argument of the Two Treatises of Government, Cambridge University Press, 1994.

Macpherson, C.B. : Introduction to Hobbes 'Leviathan, Harmondsworth, Penguins, 1968.

Marx, K.H.: The Communist Manifesto, Moscow, Progress Publishers, 1975.

McClellan, D. : The Thought of Karl Marx, London, Macmillan, 1971.

Morrow, J.: History of Political Thought: A Thematic Introduction, London, Macmillan, 1998.

Mukherjee, S. and Ramaswamy, S. : A history of Socialist Thought: From the Precursors to the Present, New Delhi, Sage, 2000.

MUKHERJEE SUBRATA AND RAMASWAMY SUSHILA: A History of Political Thoughts (Plato to Marx), 2011.

Mulgan, R.G :Aristotle's Political Theory : An Introduction for Students of Political Theory, Oxford, Clarendon Press, 1977.

Osborn, A.M. : Rousseau and Burke, New York, Simon & Schuster, 1940.

Raphael, D.D. : Problems of Political Philosophy, 2nd Ed., London, Macmillan, 1990.

RAO V.VENKATA: A History of Political Theories, 1993.

R. NELSON BRIAN: Western Political Thoughts (Socrates to the Age of Ideology), 2011.

Sabine, G.H. : What is Political Theory? Journal of Politics Vol. 1(1), pp. 1-16, 1939.

Schumpeter, J. : Capitalism, Socialism and Democracy, London, Allen &Unwin, 1976.

Strauss, L. : The Political of Hobbes: Its Basis and Genesis, Oxford, Clarendon Press, 1936.

Tannenbaum, D.G. and Schultz, D. : Inventors of Ideas, An introduction to Western Political Philosophy, New York, St. Martin's Press, 1998.

Thorson, T.L. : Plato: Totalitarian or Democrat? New Jersey, Prentice Hall, 1963.

Viroli, M. : Machiavelli, Oxford, Oxford University Press, 1998.

Wood, N. : Machiavelli, Encyclopedia of Social Sciences, London, Macmillan, 1968.

Zeller, E. : Outlines of the History of Greek Philosophy, New York, Meridian, 1955.